RESILIENT

LESSONS LEARNED, LIVES CHANGED

RESILIENT

LESSONS LEARNED, LIVES CHANGED

KATHY COOVER

CO-FOUNDER OF ISAGENIX INTERNATIONAL, LLC

ISAGENIX.

This book is dedicated to my family
who has been by my side through the
good times and hard times.
To my father who poured greatness into me
and to my mother who taught me
how to be classy.

To my husband Jim who has always been there
for me and encouraged me to go for it.
To Erik and Peta who give so much love and support.
They are my everything. They are my why.

To my greater Isagenix family who
inspire me to serve, and most importantly
to my beautiful grandchildren,
Sol and Pax, who bring me so much joy.

I will love you all forever.

CONTENTS

CHAPTER 2:
Be a Visionary

CHAPTER 3:
Be Willing to Ask

CHAPTER 4:
Have Courage

CHAPTER 5:

Have a Bold and Daring Goal

CHAPTER 6:

Do "The Do"

CHAPTER 7:

Do Good While Doing Well

INTRODUCTION

It's not what I expected would happen to me, I thought, as the doctor quietly explained my diagnosis and began to detail the aggressive treatment they had planned for me.

It was cancer. And they wanted to do an immediate hysterectomy.

But that doesn't really happen to 18 year olds... does it?

Shaken and numb, but determined to get through whatever happened next, I began searching for treatment options that would spare me from the horrible surgery I knew would change my life. As the nauseating days turned into weeks, I proactively investigated what more I could do—not just to get back to normal and emerge cancer-free, but to really experience radiant good health and enjoy a vital new energy.

Thank God for my mom, Gloria.

She investigated alternative treatments for me, and eventually, I went to UCLA Medical Center where they did an experimental procedure. Then, my stepfather—a doctor—started me on massive doses of Vitamin C and Vitamin B17.

Six months later, the magic happened.

I went in for a check up and, to my doctor's surprise, I was cancer-free. It made me a believer: the body can help itself. And what's more, I've never had a recurrence.

What began as that early bout of cancer ultimately led to a lifelong passion for health and for bringing the same kind of dramatic health transformation to others.

What does it take to overcome a life-threatening illness and eventually build a large health and wellness company? This book will reveal not just the journey, but the extraordinary people I've met along the way—and the even more profound lessons I learned as the path to success rolled out in front of me.

Long before Isagenix was even an idea, I worked as a dental hygienist in my early 20's where, day after day, the physical toll and limited income made me question how much longer I could do that work. But it also led me to wonder what more I could do to impact people's lives in a bigger way.

The idea of being more, doing more, and having more—of everything —drove me to look for new opportunities constantly. One evening, my husband Jim suggested I attend a meeting about a new product and business that was looking for new associates. Intrigued but skeptical—interested, but hesitant—I returned home and talked to him about joining up and making it my new career. I knew I had the drive to succeed and a passion for helping people. *Perhaps this is the path I've been looking for,* I thought.

It was.

Within six months, I was a leader in that company—making more than I was as a hygienist. I loved the fact that I was not only helping people improve their health, but also giving them an equal chance to create the extra income I knew would change their lives. Finally, the timing felt right for me to leave the dental profession.

Life was good in the network-marketing industry, and my dream of retiring Jim from the corporate side of the industry started to happen.

It was my first taste of real success.

But as you'll discover over the next few chapters, the business I built back then—and the lifestyle that others built with me in those days—would pale in comparison to the success and opportunity that over a million people have realized in the health and wellness company I eventually cofounded.

Isagenix.

Little did I realize 28 years ago that the dream I held of being more, having more and doing more would mean being more courageous, having more goals, doing more for others, and lifting up more families in countless cities around the world.

I'll share more of this dream in the coming pages of this book—and the stories, too. Today, my ultimate calling of impacting people's lives has become a reality, and I'm more passionate about this calling with every day that passes. It's what I live for. And, through the pages of *Resilient,* I hope you'll begin to see a 'life of more' emerging for your own future, too.

CHAPTER 1:

Be Determined

*"Anything worth doing
well is worth doing badly
in the beginning."*

—MARSHALL THURBER
Business consultant and author

She'll never make it, announced the owner of the network-marketing company to the three other, highly successful people who were in the room to be founders of this promising new start-up.

Though I had successfully opened the first dental hygiene center in California at a young age, he thought of me—not as an entrepreneur with drive and intelligence—but as a dental hygienist without talent or determination.

I was humiliated.

This humiliation made me think of my dad who had instilled in me the confidence that I could do anything I put my mind to. He had taught me that I had the talent to do anything. Remembering his encouragement brought new determination to my path.

I'll show you, I said under my breath to the owner and the other leaders in the room. And I did.

EVERYTHING IN LIFE IS A LESSON

What is required to achieve tremendous success in our industry? During my first awkward months as an associate with my very first company, I hadn't a clue. I didn't have a sponsor—except for the company itself—so I had to figure out everything on my own: presenting, recruiting, supporting others, and focusing on those activities with the biggest payoff. I was relentless to succeed.

To learn how to succeed, I studied other successful people—leaders who were earning what I wanted to earn. I created my own tools and systems to build my business. Back then, we sent out audio-cassette tapes to prospective associates. I also wrote a training book, and I taught people not only what to say but how to close. I created a voice- and fax-on-demand system for my team so they could learn and leverage these same skills and become successful.

Within six months, I was making enough to retire from my part-time job at the dentist's office and commit full-time to growing my team. I'd never had that kind of time freedom before, and I poured every minute into developing my new career.

I traveled all over the United States, holding meetings for prospective new associates and hosting trainings for those who were on board with me already. My husband—*Thank God for him*—mentored and encouraged me to keep charging forward, and soon I became the #1 income earner, creating ten separate successful teams.

Yet the owner—who had belittled and humiliated me that day—had nothing to say. No gratitude, no congratulations. Just a two-paragraph letter one day announcing he had decided to sell the company.

What! *Why?*

And where did that leave me?

Stunned and apprehensive, I learned the first of many life lessons I would acquire during times like these: *Everything in life is a lesson—whether it's accomplishing something, failing greatly, or getting your future rearranged for you, out of the blue.*

The key is to never look back. Only look forward. Learn from your mistakes, leverage your strengths, and focus on your future. Take what you have learned and move on.

And that is exactly what I did.

---

*"Closing circles, shutting doors, finishing chapters,
it doesn't matter what we call it; what matters is to leave
in the past those moments in life that are over."*

—PAUL COELHO
Brazilian author of The Alchemist

BLESSINGS IN DISGUISE

Having the rug pulled out from under you, I discovered, is almost a rite of passage for successful entrepreneurs. Of course I'd read the biographies of great and famous people. Most derived their wealth from starting and running their own businesses. Yet, almost without exception, every one of them had hit a wall—just as I was hitting a wall with the owner selling out and handing over my future to a group of investors who neither knew what I had accomplished, or cared about what I could do with the business I had built.

What's worse, I began to question their integrity. The day after the company was acquired, they faxed me a new compensation plan that cut my income down to virtually nothing. Knowing I couldn't stay, I sold my organization to someone who I knew would take care of my people and help them grow their own incomes. It was time to move on.

Within weeks, I had researched and found another company where I knew I'd do well. Though I was the newest female in a company of mostly men, my experience with building organizations, training people, and creating systems paid off: I quickly became the fastest person ever to reach Diamond position and join the company's top ranks. Once again I created many of the systems and tools I needed to grow my team and support others in growing theirs, only now it was much easier: I had the skills and experience I'd acquired over years of doing the same thing elsewhere.

But now the stakes were higher.

As many successful women do in this industry, I'd "retired" my husband from his corporate job. For years, Jim had given me his unwavering support. I knew that I couldn't have achieved all this without him. After years of being my biggest cheerleader, I thought, he deserved to take time to explore what he wanted to do next—if anything. We also had a son, Erik, and the financial responsibility for our family, our household, and our future was now all on me.

I became relentless, both in my immediate goal of reaching the top rank and in my longer term goal of making an impact in people's lives. Long before modern technology existed like Google or Maps, I flew to New Jersey, rented a car, and drove city-to-city down the Eastern seaboard. New York, Baltimore, Washington DC, Richmond. Meeting after meeting, I made the case for taking charge of one's financial future and creating new-found time freedom—all backed by the power of a company doing the heavy-lifting of product development, administration, and fulfillment.

I did conference calls from pay phones. I used an old-fashioned overhead projector to illustrate the compensation plan. And I did meetings with people I had never met before—all by myself. It was scary sometimes, being a woman alone on the road by myself. But the hard work paid off: within 18 months, not only had I exceeded my personal income goal, but I had finally reached the rank of Double Diamond—an achievement that came with a very large check. I remember being so excited. For weeks, I was joyful and grateful.

Then, during a routine call to the company to check my weekly numbers, a stranger answered the phone and said the company had been shut down by government officials. *A regulatory matter,* they said. I was devastated. All that work...all that income...all those families, households, lives, and futures that I had improved and changed were now on uncertain ground because someone had failed to consult the lawyers and stay above board.

It was a life lesson I'll never forget: tell the truth, follow the rules, and listen to your legal team. These lessons were about to become priceless.

THE FIRST RESPONSE WHEN LIFE HAPPENS

While it would have been easy to despair when my livelihood disappeared, I'd learned by then that staying positive is the most important thing you can do. Practicing gratitude is the second most important.

Once again, I pursued another network-marketing business (this was in the travel industry), and once again it failed: on September 11, 2001—a day I will never forget for the rest of my life—I saw not only the horror on television, but I saw my business get shattered, too.

"Enough!" I said.

I was not going to do this again. No more company leadership, no more mistakes, no more team members whose dreams of a better life I'd supported and helped grow—dreams that were now shattered along with mine. Instead of finding another company, I wanted to start my own business and train others on how to be successful in the network-marketing industry.

With free time on my hands, I pursued a class that literally changed my life. It was a 45-day challenge to improve in every way: health, family, relationships, and spirituality. For the first time in years, I actually had some time to work on myself.

And, in the process, I learned a lot about me.

Part of the 45-day challenge was to express gratitude every day to family members, friends, business associates, and others.

One morning, as I was making breakfast for Erik, I told him how grateful I was that he was my son. At the time, he was 13, and he looked at me like I was a little crazy. I kept going on and on about how grateful and proud of him I was. Now looking back, it was one of the best things I ever did for my relationship with him.

Even today, he still mentions to others, "My mom believes in me. She texts me messages of gratitude."

It made a huge impact on him as a teenager and helped develop the wonderful relationship we have today.

That 45-day lesson in gratitude is one I've never forgotten. And I still maintain a gratitude practice today. It's made a big difference in my life. In fact, I'm convinced that staying positive and having gratitude through those "days in limbo" ultimately helped prepare me to launch Isagenix.

GOOD VS. GREAT: IT'S ALWAYS YOUR CHOICE

Have you ever been in situation when your job, a relationship, or an opportunity suddenly ends, and you think it's the end of the world—but suddenly, an exciting new doorway opens in front of you?

I've been there. Several times.

And what I've discovered is that, often, the thing that's holding you back from an incredible future needs to fall away before that future can show up fully. We only have so much bandwidth in our lives. When we hold onto a bad relationship or stay in a lackluster job or doggedly pursue a mediocre opportunity, we don't have the extra time, energy or focus to dedicate to something new. We're so focused on the "good," there's no available space in our lives for the "great" to show up.

In my own life, starting three businesses, focusing on growing them, and earning over a million dollars a year was good. But they were only a preview of the greater success I was about to create with Isagenix. These "successful" endeavors *had to go,* so that my greater future could begin to take shape.

In the same way, time and again, I've seen other people's lives transformed after some "disaster" occurred, when—in hindsight—that disaster was actually a blessing in disguise: it was a necessary clearing away of the merely good, so the great had a chance show up.

By this point in my life, I was seriously considering my future. I felt there was still so much left to do. I had a sense of responsibility to the profession that I loved. And while I didn't want to start another team, I realized that I had learned so much—and there was so much to share with others. I knew that if we could control our future and do everything with the right intentions, the magic would happen. We could create a spectacular future, I thought, for everyone. Isagenix was that future.

"With the new day comes new strengths
and new thoughts."

—ELEANOR ROOSEVELT
Longest-serving First Lady of the United States, diplomat and activist

---

ALWAYS STAY TRUE TO YOUR DREAMS

Have you ever had a dream so powerful that you had no idea how you would accomplish it? Have you ever known there was something bigger in your future, but you didn't quite know how to get there?

After my last company crashed, I admit I was almost ready to give up. Though I'd spent over 10 years in this industry inspiring other people to build their own teams, to persevere and never quit, I actually believed the best thing for my future was to end my career as a leader and start a training company—somewhere, I didn't know where—to help others learn about the network-marketing profession.

There was no question that I had developed unique knowledge and expertise, with the added benefit of operating at the top of numerous companies. I had learned how to treat people. I'd learned how to work with people. I learned to speak in front of vast audiences. I learned how to embrace each company and the network-marketing field as a whole.

And yet every new venture had ended in disaster. *Why?* Was this some kind of message the Universe was trying to send me? Or were these disappointments simply preparing me for my bigger future? I didn't know the answer, but the 45-day challenge class I talked about earlier gave me the space I needed to consider what I wanted to do.

Little did I know the unexpected shift in my thinking that would occur.

For one thing, the instructor teaching the class began to believe in me in ways that, given the last several years, I couldn't do on my own.

"You're *the best* at network marketing," he said at the completion of the class. "You should start your own company."

About the same time, Jim and I were approached by a nutraceutical pioneer, John Anderson, who had already formulated over 2,000 products for 600 companies. Not only that, but he also owned a network-marketing company that wasn't going the way he wanted.

Jim and I had just moved into our dream house in Scottsdale, when the phone rang. The caller ID read "John Anderson."

"Hmm. Do you know somebody named John Anderson?" I asked Jim.

"Don't answer it!" he replied. "He wants us to go to work for him."

But John was persistent, and after the phone rang several more times, I picked it up.

"Kathy? Hi. Could you and Jim come over and have dinner with my wife and me?"

That night, meeting with John, we saw his commitment to creating no-compromise wellness products and were convinced that together we could create something special.

We decided to join him and soon found ourselves sitting around a conference table, asking questions and giving John ideas. Why are so many people overweight? Why are so many people unhealthy?

All of a sudden, John got a look in his eyes and said, "I have it. I know what we need to do."

He left, saying, "I'll have the formulations done in two days."

"Really," Jim and I said, giving each other the side-eye.

But two days later, John presented us with a complete wellness system of four products that would start our journey.

Finally, here was the opportunity I'd been preparing for my entire career.

It would give us a chance to build a company that was different: one that took care of its people, and that you could count on to be a legacy for your family and your future—where you didn't have to worry whether the company would suddenly change the compensation plan or make a mistake and go out of business.

It would allow us to design the compensation plan in a way that no other company had ever done. Having been in the trenches for years, we knew what worked and what didn't. We could finally reward hard work and consistent effort. We could reward people for doing more of the right things: duplicating themselves and empowering others. And this time around, things would be different: no surprises, no shattering people's dreams in an instant. In fact, I knew the company would be well capitalized to weather any business storm.

Not only that, but it would put us in a unique position to make a difference in people's health, as well as their wealth.

Jim said, "Let's take this vehicle that we love called network marketing, and let's fulfill the promise of what this industry can be. We can create a community of people with a positive culture—not one based on uncertainty or fear. And if we do it right, the right people will show up."

We would build it into the most trusted and respected company in the industry for decades to come—a company deserving of the thousands of letters sent every year by people whose financial futures have been changed and whose words often bring me to tears.

Plus, we could build a company that focused on changing lives in so many more ways than just helping people earn an exciting income. We could focus on improving people's health and wellness, and on creating new lifestyles for millions of families around the world. Hardworking parents would have time to spend with their children again. Entire communities could be strengthened as the new company helped lift people out of illness, poverty and despair.

Because of the quality of the products, we also realized that, once we went global, Isagenix could contribute to better health for entire countries around the world—many of whose healthcare systems are going broke trying to treat health issues that could have been prevented with proper nutrition. We wanted to be at the leading edge of people taking control of their own health—taking preventative action with science-based products that get results that you can't find anywhere else.

Our modern world has become so toxic. We knew that, in order for people to absorb the great nutrition our shakes provide, we needed to first help people detoxify their bodies. And while we still have a lot of work to do to reach around the globe, we still believe—as we did back then—that the most important thing was to start with high quality nutrition in a low-calorie system that people could easily incorporate into their lifestyle.

We can change world health with that simple plan, we thought.

It was a big vision with a big impact.

With these goals in mind and with the early planning of Isagenix now underway, I began to realize that everything that I'd experienced in the past—the successes, the disappointments, the fast growth, even the humiliation and the stress of sudden disruptions—had systematically prepared me for the exciting challenge of building Isagenix.

There was no looking back. There was only moving forward.

"Don't dwell on what went wrong.
Instead, focus on what to do next."

—DENIS WAITLEY
Bestselling author of The Psychology of Winning

WHAT YOU'VE HEARD IS TRUE:
EVERYTHING HAPPENS FOR A REASON

Of all the Isagenix associates I've met and mentored over the years, Zach Slobin is someone who's lived this principle over and over again. For years, he was a serial entrepreneur living through one "rite of passage" after another.

In fact, if *Resilient* had been a book 20 years ago, Zach Slobin could have written it. Growing up with the dream—and the talent—of becoming a star athlete, Zach's father ingrained in him a sense of destiny early in his life.

"Like unrefined clay waiting to become a great sculpture," reminisced Zach. And for a while, in his 20's, that path seemed to beckon with a bright future. But somehow, his life began to take all the wrong turns.

When athletics didn't work out, he decided to pursue a future in entrepreneurship. Everything he touched seemed to succeed. He excelled in the real estate industry in the early days of equity insurance and sold millions. He built a customer base in the artisan coffee business that eclipsed his earlier success. And later, in the real-estate education market, where his natural affinity for teaching and developing people made him a popular leader, he was a rock star earning more than ever. Entrepreneurship—and the network-marketing model—had repeatedly paid off big for Zach.

Yet with each success, Zach's triumphs were defeated by business partners who threw him under the bus, companies that suddenly went out of business, and ethical issues that forced him to simply leave.

In the midst of these professional losses, Zach's personal life was also in shambles. After three years with his fiancée, they both came to the conclusion they weren't good for each other.

"I was suicidal after the breakup," Zach admits. "I battled depression. And after each loss—business or personal—I'd lay on the couch, feeling powerless and smoking weed."

To get himself going again, he launched a marketing and training company serving network-marketing leaders from different companies. He knew technology was the future, and he knew how to help leaders grow their organizations with the latest online tools. While a friend had introduced him to Isagenix and he liked the products, Zach felt that he had turned his back on the network-marketing industry for good.

His girlfriend Eden, meanwhile, (now his wife) was focused on clean living: organic food, a plant-based diet, low-stress living. When a dream trip to Vietnam caused her to look for a product she could take with her to ensure access to safe food and clean nutrition, Zach handed her his Isagenix shake mix.

Eden was thrilled.

In fact, after a two-week trip in Asia with no jet lag and boundless energy, she urged Zach to get started and build a team. "Or I will," she said.

Wondering if he were crazy, Zach attended an Isagenix meeting where I happened to be that night.

He's got battle scars just like me, I thought when I first met him.

"Are you open to me showing you how different Isagenix can be?" I asked. "Isagenix will never let you down."

And it never has.

What struck me so forcibly when I first met Zach is how closely his story resembled mine: serial entrepreneurship and never-ending let-downs. Yet through it all, Zach continually looked for the open doorway. He eventually came to realize that business blow-ups, failed relationships, and starting over were just a chance to learn more, get more experience, and be prepared for when real opportunity showed up. He realized that the people who were in the way—those "good" activities which were stealing his time—actually *removed themselves* from his life so he had time to pursue the great.

WHAT YOU WANT IS JUST BEYOND
THE POINT OF QUITTING

One of the most interesting truths in life is that success and failure go hand-in-hand. If you're not failing—at least in the beginning—it means you're not working hard enough on succeeding. Every great inventor, scientist, businessperson, athlete—you name it—has failed *many times* on the road to greatness. In fact, stories abound of famous people who experienced colossal failure just before achieving the breakthrough success that eventually defined their life and legacy.

The key is: they didn't quit.

In my own life, there were many times when I could have quit. Goodness knows, I wanted to. For instance, in the early days, one of my biggest fears was speaking in front of a roomful of people. Small groups or large, it didn't matter. Usually, my fear was so intense that I would actually leave the room when I thought someone would call on me to speak.

Then the day came when I had to do my first presentation in front of 100 people. I'd practiced repeatedly with my son Erik who patiently listened to my speech over and over again. By the time I finally went on stage, my hands were sweating. Then I got so cold and started shivering so badly that my teeth began chattering. Still, I started speaking and somehow made it through. When it was over, one of my dearest friends came up to me and said, "Kathy, you were SO bad. But I still love you!"

I wanted to die and throw in the towel. What's worse, I knew I would never make it in this industry if I couldn't speak publicly and train others to do what I did. But miraculously, after that one terrifying experience, the fear faded away!

As each event approached where I knew I'd be called on to speak, I'd practice in front of the bathroom mirror until I felt more confident and the fear of speaking just went away.

"Quitting because you don't want to be uncomfortable will prevent you from growing."

—AMY MORIN
Psychotherapist and international bestselling author of
13 Things Mentally Strong People Don't Do

EVERY REASON IN THE WORLD TO QUIT, BUT SEVEN PRECIOUS REASONS NOT TO

One of the most enjoyable things about my work is getting to know many of our amazing leaders. I also have the honor of reaching out to people who have achieved a certain benchmark in Isagenix.

One story that I hold near to my heart is Deanna Falchook's. When I called to congratulate her on earning $20,000* in our leadership pool, she burst into tears and was so grateful. Hers is a story that needs to be told.

---

* *Results not typical.*

As a successful singer in New York—with her own dance band and dozens of bookings a year from Disney, The Trump Organization, society weddings and more—Deanna Falchook knew what an amazing life looked like. She was surrounded by opulence at the private homes and expensive wedding venues where she performed, and dreamed one day of living the same way.

But when the economy crashed in 2008 and private parties with professional entertainers dwindled, her dreams of opulence—and even the comfortable lifestyle she was already living—came to a halt.

The Great Recession hit hard. But it didn't just impact Deanna.

A few years before, at the height of her career, Deanna and her husband Mark had started a family, raising two beautiful children. They'd also adopted a baby from Guatemala and, a few years later, three young children from Ethiopia who needed the love, stability and future that Deanna and Mark could provide. Later, they brought home a son from Ukraine. Yet by 2012, with her husband finding only part-time work, the Falchooks were facing foreclosure and their precious children were officially on the poverty grid: the first step to qualifying for Medicaid and other government assistance. Day by day, Deanna's world narrowed to just those tasks that would keep her family from falling further into despair. When she eventually had to turn to a local food pantry for free groceries, she knew they'd hit rock bottom.

"It was my moment of quiet desperation," she recalls. "I even began to wonder, *If these children hadn't been adopted, would life be better for them?*"

At that moment, Deanna wept and began to pray: *God, scour the Universe for an opportunity to help me support these kids.*

Within days, an acquaintance suggested Isagenix, an idea that made Deanna instantly balk. "Why would God send that?" she remembers thinking. "I thought He would send something that would help me make money and stay at home with the kids."

But for days, she couldn't get the idea out of her head. *Maybe my biases about network marketing are wrong,* she thought. Maybe she *could* be successful with Isagenix, as other people were.

Though Deanna didn't know network marketing, she did have a network:

the parents of other adopted children whom she'd met online. Often, their children had come from desperate circumstances or suffered malnutrition during infancy. These kids needed good nutrition even more than other children did. And nearly every adoptive family, Deanna knew, needed post-adoption financial aid—something that didn't exist.

While Deanna could have said no to the opportunity, she knew deep-down that bringing her family out of their desperate financial circumstances required saying yes. *How many people linger in desperation and just stay there,* she thought, *wanting a way out, but never making an effort to do so?*

While Deanna had every reason to quit—every opportunity to say no—she didn't. And within months, she had one of the fastest growing teams in Isagenix.

Today, Deanna and her husband are on top of the world, living their dream lifestyle in Florida, traveling the world with other Isagenix leaders, and bringing better nutrition—and the stability of wealth—to thousands of families everywhere.

Sometimes, climbing out of your circumstances requires you to climb out of your comfort zone. It requires you to keep going when quitting is so much easier.

WHAT HAPPENS WHEN YOUR "WHY" KEEPS YOU FROM QUITTING

One of the beautiful parts of our business is the people we meet. Another story I love—about someone who didn't quit—is the story of Karla Italiano whose "why" was her biggest motivation. The very first time I met this lady was on an incentive trip—she had earned her first cruise to Europe.

She had a beautiful energy and light that attracted people to her. She wanted to impact people's lives and make a difference. Her smile was infectious. And as I got to know her, I sensed that there was something very special about her.

It's leukemia, said the pediatric specialist who'd been recommended to Karla and her husband Pasquale. For months, they'd suspected something was wrong as, day after day, their five-year-old daughter weakened.

Three years earlier, Karla had been a successful engineer with a Master's degree and a department of her own. She regularly traveled for work—Atlanta, Los Angeles, Santiago—and had high-level mentors who supported and guided her career. With noticeable intelligence and a stand-out work ethic, Karla was repeatedly promoted at work, moving up the corporate ladder with impressive speed. Yet with every promotion, her work hours grew and she lost more and more time for her young family.

Soon, her twin daughters would be old enough to enter pre-school. And Karla wanted the best for them. Yet private school would require a bigger income, and as for the daily school run and other activities—Karla simply didn't have the time.

Wondering what she could do to earn more money and have more time freedom, Karla got a call from a friend about a network-marketing opportunity. While her first try sapped her confidence in the industry, she soon realized that keeping her children in private school and being home for her daughters was a bigger reason to stick with the idea. Her "why" wouldn't let her quit.

Then she discovered Isagenix.

At her very first Isagenix event, she got a vision of what she could earn. Her confidence—which had been low—began to soar. Even when her friends said no to Isagenix, Karla talked to strangers. When her first conversation caused the prospect to walk away (literally), she still was determined. Though it made so much sense to quit, Karla knew her girls were counting on her to stay in their school and come home to a mom who was there for them. Day after day, the story played in her head about all the reasons to quit. But Karla's "why" wouldn't let her quit. She set a 30-day goal at first, then bigger goals in time. And after three and a half years of daily discipline, Karla Italiano became one of the top leaders in the company.

She had created time freedom and a substantial income.

But now, one of the twins needed her desperately. With a leukemia diagnosis, she would eventually need 25 months of chemotherapy and spend 43 nights in the hospital before she battled the childhood cancer into remission. Through it all, with the steady income from her Isagenix business, Karla had the ability to step away from her daily disciplines and be with her daughter full-time.

"If we want to feel an undying passion for our work, if we want to feel we are contributing to something bigger than ourselves, we all need to know our WHY."

—SIMON SINEK
Bestselling author of Start With Why and Leaders Eat Last

YOUR "WHY" WILL CREATE A SPECTACULAR FUTURE…IF YOU LET IT

Just as Karla Italiano learned, your "why" can inspire you to create a spectacular future. It can keep you focused on your goals. It can give you a vision of what's ahead. But most importantly, it can remind you of what you can really do with your life if you set your mind to it.

One of my favorite pastimes is to read the biographies and study the advice of business greats who experienced downfall, yet never gave up. They've helped me create my own checklist of success strategies that, over the years, have helped me emerge from times of unexpected defeat and career disaster. Even today, my mantra is, *Always be learning.*

These lessons, in addition to the curveballs that my own life has thrown me, guide my steps and remind me that building something big and impacting people's lives is a matter of mindset over circumstances. What tips have I learned and followed?

Saying No to the Good Makes Room for the Great

In his book, *Good to Great,* author Jim Collins tells us, "Good is the enemy of great." What I like to say is that focusing on merely good opportunities or being satisfied with merely good outcomes actually keeps us from living a life of greatness. In fact, holding onto the "good"—like that good job we hate or that good relationship we're loyal to—actually keeps great opportunities waiting in the wings. Even worse, many of us get caught up in pursuing second-rate opportunities we think will bring us the life we want, but which actually rob us of the time and focus needed to do those things necessary to bring about the achievement we want.

To help me say no to the good, so I have time and energy to say yes to the great, there's a mental checklist I use:

- Does this opportunity fit with my overall life purpose and passion?
- Is it more hassle than it's worth?
- Have I gathered all the information I need?
- Could I test it out with a small amount of money and time?
- And most importantly, has someone else done this successfully?

What Others Think of You Is Not What Will Really Happen

Too often we live in a world of "what if's." We take a comment that someone's made about us—or an opinion they have—and we apply it our own life as if that person has a crystal ball and knows our future.

They don't.

But when we live our lives based upon what other people think of us, it influences our decisions. A single comment can make us suddenly feel less capable or less worthy of success. It can make us less likely to take the steps needed to achieve our goal. But, just like that company owner who belittled me in the conference room all those years ago, what others think of you *is not what will really happen.*

Their opinions about what you're doing or about the goals you've made for your life *simply don't matter.* It's up to you to create your own future—just as it's your responsibility to ignore what others say in judgment.

Learn to Fail Successfully

One of my favorite stories is about Thomas Edison who failed more than 1,000 times before successfully inventing the electric light bulb. When a reporter asked him, "How did it feel to fail 1,000 times?" Edison replied, "I didn't fail 1,000 times. The light bulb was an invention with 1,000 steps."

We too can look at "failure" as a positive learning experience in our own lives. Instead of being afraid to fail (which often keeps us from starting in the first place), we can look at any new pursuit as a way to become smarter, more experienced and more confident. Simply start, make mistakes, ask others how to do it better, modify your approach, and keep going.

CHAPTER 2:

Be a Visionary

"The visionary starts with a clean piece of paper and re-imagines the world."

—MALCOLM GLADWELL
New York Times bestselling author of The Tipping Point:
How Little Things Can Make a Big Difference

One of the earliest lessons I learned in those first few months of launching Isagenix is that *momentum is contagious.* Everything that happens in life is a lesson—whether it's a successful effort, a mistake that we've made, or something that's happened to us that's outside our control. We must all learn from our past and move forward with determination.

In those first busy months, that's exactly what I had committed to do.

With John working on product development and Jim helping to structure the compensation plan and the company, I went to work reaching out to early leaders, developing training materials, and hosting events. I called everyone I knew and shared my excitement for what we were creating. Many bought into our vision and joined us—and their lives have been forever changed.

It was the kind of busy, exhausting, but equally rewarding growth that reminded me of what futurist and inventor Buckminster Fuller once explained: your life is like a speedboat moving through the water. Behind you is a wake of activity and accomplishment that will not only inspire and attract others—but will positively impact their lives. While you may never hear about it, your actions will eventually impact millions.

Just like that speedboat, our job is to *be in motion.*

And I was.

GROWING A BUSINESS REQUIRES
GROWING ITS PEOPLE

To help get our earliest leaders trained quickly, I launched the first Isagenix University where I created the content, did all the training and even set up the room by myself. It was exhausting, but I knew it was necessary for success.

Later, as we evolved, we asked Isagenix leaders who were having success to do the training—giving the events new-found energy as others shared their stories.

We brought in David T. S. Wood—a sought-out success trainer and personal-growth coach—to develop our associates as individuals who would set goals, stay focused, and face down their fears. It made a huge difference, and it taught me something: you're only as great as you can grow as a person.

David used accelerated-learning techniques, and it made a huge impact on how people learned. More leaders started emerging among people who had never been in network marketing before: mechanics, school teachers, stay-at-home moms, military women. We knew we had something special when we could teach the average person to be successful at this.

I knew that if we did things like our lives depended on it, we would create the kind of "contagious momentum" that would attract not just new associates, but top network-marketing professionals who were displaced or disenchanted at their current companies.

For years, I'd taught that you don't have to be "big" yet to attract others. Your belief and determination will be obvious.

Lynn Hagedorn Clouse is someone who started fast and kept moving.

I will never forget the day Lynn walked into our office. She'd been in network marketing with another company, but something was missing.

Lynn is one of those beautiful, heartfelt women who has the power to move people. I went through the compensation plan with her on the whiteboard. I remember taking my shoes off and getting right into the power of our plan. After she saw the depth we paid on an organization—and all the upfront money that was available—she was more than interested.

"I have to do this," she told me. "I have to replace my income fast."

"Then you need to do this like your life depends on it," I replied.

Almost overnight, she did. As soon as we mapped out her plan, she went to work calling everyone she knew! As she passionately invited other leaders to join her, Lynn quickly rose to the top of the company.

DO MORE IN LESS TIME

If you ever go to Nebraska, you'll see mile after mile of cornfields, farmland, and the wide Missouri River. It's America's heartland... The Great Plains. Growing up in Omaha, Lynn inherited good Midwestern values and a strong work ethic. She was also the quiet shy kid. But Lynn had something that even shyness couldn't contain: ambition and a heart for helping people.

She had earned her degree as an occupational therapist and then went on to earn her Master's degree. But she quickly learned that, in her chosen profession, she was only going to go so far. When she discovered network marketing, she was at the peak of her career and in the busiest time of her life, raising three kids under the age of eight. She talked up the idea of network marketing to friends, but decided early on that it wasn't for her.

"I had too many initials after my name," recalls Lynn. "I was a health practitioner with a degree and the certifications to go with it. I thought network marketing was beneath me."

Then a friend, who recognized Lynn was working long hours in a career that would always limit her pay, urged Lynn to take another look at network marketing. More importantly, she shared specifically why she believed it would work for Lynn.

What if, thought Lynn. *What if this is the thing that will change my life?*

Joining a company that looked promising, she quickly began holding meetings in her house, working hard to grow her team, and looking for others who would build fast, too. For awhile, she was happy with her results. She learned a lot and grew as a person.

But eventually, Lynn realized the company was missing something that would truly help her achieve the financial success she wanted. So, she spent the next two years researching other companies to pursue instead... which led her to Isagenix.

Lynn was so intrigued, she decided to fly to the corporate headquarters in Arizona to meet the Isagenix team and check things out.

"I was looking for a forever home," remembers Lynn. "When I toured Isagenix and met Kathy, I realized I'd found the company I'd been searching for—they seemed to be doing everything right."

What Lynn saw—along with her vision of what she could do—was so strong that she resigned her position in the other company and instantly took her household income to zero.

Now her back was against the wall.

Lynn went home from that visit to Arizona and put into practice a simple technique she'd previously learned—*success compression*: do more in less time. While most associates might talk to 10 people in a week or a month, Lynn talked to 10 people before noon. Her cordless phone would die, and she'd pick up another one. Just like a pilot who is judged by time in the cockpit instead of years on the job, Lynn invested more time, effort, and energy into building her business that first year than probably anyone else in the history of Isagenix.

And in that first year, she won every award. Plus, she went on to become the fastest person ever to earn $1 million: it took her just 14 months.*

"The passion, momentum and excitement you bring when you are building fast is highly attractive to people," Lynn says. "When you have a posture of confidence and a clear vision of where you're going, people want to be a part of it."

I want that in my life, they say.

Starting in July of 2011, Lynn replaced her former income in just 90 days—and by the end of the year, she'd surpassed it. Over the years, Lynn and her husband Michael have combined to earn close to $20 million in Isagenix.*

Today, Lynn and Michael passionately pour themselves into their ever-growing worldwide team. They love looking down into their organization —even 200 or more levels down—hoping to find someone who has that *burning desire to succeed*. When they find them, they know the Isagenix compensation plan will reward them for teaching and training them how to climb to the top of the mountain, too. Lifting people up, helping them

---

* *Results not typical.*

grow, and keeping the energy high in their organization is where Lynn and Michael shine.

"Successful people are always looking for opportunities to help others. Unsuccessful people are always asking, 'What's in it for me?'."

—BRIAN TRACY
Author of more than 70 books including Earn What You're Really Worth

---

A TIDAL WAVE OF GROWTH

With early successes at Isagenix beginning to create a stir in the network-marketing industry, recognized leaders at other companies were starting to leave their organizations to jump on Isagenix's tidal wave of growth. They were looking for a company with values, something they could count on—something that would be there for their children.

At the same time, our own "homegrown" leaders were starting to emerge. People began showing up in a much bigger way. And since I knew that everything—growth, impact, success—depended upon individual leaders, we worked hard to support them and help them become visionaries within their own teams. We also asked them to join us in our goal to impact world health.

Slowly, that vision started to become a reality.

Of course, none of this would have been possible in those early days without the outstanding Isagenix products that were delivering results you simply couldn't get anywhere else. It wasn't just that people were shedding extra pounds, they were detoxifying, too—something the medical profession was just starting to recognize as an important health tool.

Among the many thousands who were getting healthier on Isagenix products in those early days was a special group of people who were losing significant amounts of weight. In our first few years, we created the 100 Pound Club and now have over 700 people who have lost 100 pounds or more (and those 700 are just the people we know about). Others I meet in unusual circumstances, like the lady who ran up to me in the airport one day and raved, "My husband lost 165 pounds on your products. You saved his life!"

Story after story, these people warm my heart.

One of my favorite success stories from the early months of Isagenix emerged when I went to Nashville and did a meeting for a small group there. In these more informal settings, I always ask how many in the group have lost 10 pounds, 20, 50…100 pounds or more. This precious lady stood up and replied, "I've lost 104 pounds on your products!"

She was 77 years old and 5-foot-2-inches with her cowboy boots and hat on. "Now I'm lookin' for a younger man," she said with a wink.

Her confidence and sparkle really made my day.

RESULTS HE COULDN'T GET ANYWHERE ELSE

While people from all walks of life were getting results with Isagenix products, never in my wildest dreams did I expect a celebrity to become a top earner in the company—starting with the products alone.

John Gray, the international bestselling author of *Men Are From Mars, Women Are From Venus*, attended our very first company event: Summer Splash. While standing in the wings, waiting to go on stage, I was startled when John came up to me and said, "My name is John Gray. I'm using your products, and I feel fabulous!"

John went on to share that he'd lost 25 pounds, and he woke up and went to bed every day in a good mood. "I want to share this," he added, and within minutes, he had jumped on stage to share his excitement about the results he was getting on our product. Not only had his mental clarity improved, John reported, but his energy was off the charts. After the event, John approached me and, in his funny demeanor, asked, "So how do I do this as a business?"

"Give me three dynamic women to help you build, and I'll train them for you," I offered.

John did.

To this day, his original referrals—Ellen Bradley, Andrea Henkart, and Rhonda Coallier—are still top earners, helping John make more money from Isagenix than he does from his amazing books. Soon, John was speaking at our national events and promoting the product everywhere. But a chance conversation with his good friend, Jack Canfield, literally brought a powerful new level of training to Isagenix and proved, once again, that personal growth leads to personal achievement.

It was 2005 when we met Jack, who was world-renowned for his popular *Chicken Soup for the Soul* book series. But Jack's real passion project that year was his latest *New York Times* bestseller: *The Success Principles*—a collection of 64 principles the world's top achievers use to excel in business, athletics, philanthropy, science, the arts, and more. Jack was intrigued by the results that John Gray had experienced with Isagenix products, and he soon flew to Arizona to meet with us. Not only did that meeting begin a lifelong association with Jack—who regularly spoke at our national conventions—but it proved to me, once again, the powerful impact that personal growth training could have on our associates' success.

Together, Jack Canfield and John Gray brought not only a thirst for self-development to our associates, they brought a level of credibility to the company that was unprecedented.

KEEP GROWING YOUR VISION ONCE IT BEGINS TO TAKE OFF

With people getting results by the hundreds and new members of the 100 Pound Club being added frequently in the early days of Isagenix, we were inspired to quickly expand the Isagenix product line well beyond cleansing and weight loss. We added anti-aging products, fitness and performance products—plus we created an online wellness store so people could shop for products at their own store, then refer others, creating a growing network of people who were buying and consuming the BEST products in the world.

Isagenix truly was delivering results you cannot get from anything else. Once again, it was time to dream bigger.

In 2006, I was reading Bill Phillips' bestselling book, *Body for Life,* about a 12-week cardio and weight-lifting program that not only changed people's body, but changed their mindset, too. While gym time certainly helps, I knew that Isagenix actually provided the missing link to creating an amazing physique: detoxification and nutrition. That realization led me to launch the IsaBody Challenge—a program to support people in achieving amazing physical results as they started on the products. Thousands upon thousands of people have gone through this challenge—making it one of our hallmark programs. Other initiatives like travel incentives, special pricing and other promotions were creating new financial and lifestyle opportunities for families—giving them hope and belief in a better life.

There's no question people were making money, but we also began to see something much more transformational emerging: a health-product company that was transforming the well-being of entire populations around the globe—indigenous peoples, young families, college students, and more.

The magic had started to happen. Our original vision to impact world health was starting to take off.

"Results transform the world."

—MICHAEL GERBER
Bestselling author of Awakening the Entrepreneur Within:
How Ordinary People Can Create Extraordinary Companies

In 2007, we expanded distribution of Isagenix products into Australia, Hong Kong and New Zealand. I remember that year visiting one of the Maori communities in New Zealand and seeing first-hand the health challenges these people were living with. Women died, on average, at 55 years old. So sad. The vast majority of these indigenous people were overweight and needed the weight-loss results and better nutrition our products delivered.

As I met them one by one, they couldn't believe, at my age, how young, vibrant and healthy I looked and—most especially—the remarkable energy I had.

These people still hold a special place in my heart. So when associate Gabby Deane joined us from Australia—simply to help out her mom and dad financially by sending money back home to New Zealand—I was thrilled that the result *instead* was the beginning of a shift in the health of the indigenous Maori people of New Zealand—a beautiful country which, tragically, also has the third highest rate of obesity per capita in the world.

Gabby Deane grew up on a dairy farm where her parents worked long hours well into their 70's. In New Zealand, farmers barely make a living, and after decades of borrowing against non-existent profits, the bank threatened to force the sale of her parents' property in order to pay their longstanding debt.

Living this no-win lifestyle day after day, Gabby's parents encouraged their children to get an education and find careers away from the farm. Heartsick at the idea of leaving her blissful country home—and the only life she'd ever known—Gabby got an accounting degree and moved to New Zealand's capital city, Auckland, to work in a sterile high-rise away from the green spaces and outdoors that she loved.

Sending money home to save the family farm became Gabby's driving passion. So when an opportunity came up to move to Australia and double her salary, Gabby jumped at the chance. She soon realized, however, that her oversized paycheck came at a cost. While it allowed Gabby to send even more money home every month, she had to work 100-120 hours a week to climb the ladder at her new accounting firm—eventually earning AU$175,000.

Instead of taking vacation time to visit the farm, she worked. Instead of meeting other young people her age, she worked. Instead of doing good for others, which was a growing interest for Gabby, she worked.

Gabby was miserable. And, as it turned out, she wasn't alone: New Zealanders routinely leave their homes to seek better pay in Sydney, Melbourne, and Perth. And like many of her fellow Kiwi's, Gabby was homesick and wanted to return. Plus, as a Millennial who was single, professional, and driven, the life of "more" that she craved—more freedom, more time, more doing good for others—was literally passing her by.

When a chance client assignment in Perth led Gabby to meet Isagenix associate Peta Kelly, Gabby's life soon changed forever. At an evening event, Peta asked Gabby and the other 20-somethings in the room to write down their vision of the perfect life.

How much money do I really want? wondered Gabby. *Could I move back to New Zealand, renovate my grandma's run-down house at the beach, and go kayaking every day? And what about having a family of my own? Or traveling the world like other carefree people my age are doing?*

"If I showed you how to get that life," Peta asked, "could I have your attention for the next 30 minutes?"

While Gabby knew next to nothing about network marketing, her accounting experience told her that earning residual income would allow her to move home, travel the world, and be happy.

Here was a way to have everything she wanted—plus help other Kiwi's move home, too. And with the Isagenix products, she could literally change the health of the Pacific Islanders and Maori people of North Island whose poverty contributed to New Zealand's skyrocketing obesity rate.

It was a big vision. Yet Gabby knew that regret would haunt her if she *didn't pursue this chance* to join Isagenix and start building fast. The fear of that regret convinced her.

Within nine months, Gabby Deane quit the accounting firm and moved back to New Zealand to renovate her grandmother's beach house at Coromandel, North Island. She began a health transformation of the country's Pacific Islanders and Maori people—many of whom were low-income families or on government assistance due to poor health. Their limited income and unhealthy habits meant they often survived on cheap packaged foods, while the high cost of farmland prevented them from growing their own nutrient-rich foods. Too often they lived in state housing and relied on government benefits.

With Isagenix products, however, they've achieved astounding results. And with the Isagenix business opportunity, they've earned extra money which has raised their standard of living. Instead of working long hours at multiple jobs in order to make ends meet, their Isagenix income has let them quit jobs that were negatively impacting their health or family life.

Not only that, but Gabby has devoted herself to ending the poverty and poor nutrition that used to be passed down from generation to generation. Sadly, New Zealand has one of world's highest rates of childhood obesity. Children who don't have a good education can't get good jobs later. But Gabby is working to end this cycle by helping to educate families on the importance of a healthy diet for their children while giving them nutritious options like Isagenix products.

After tackling her goals in New Zealand, Gabby spent a year traveling the world—her dream come true—connecting with Isagenix associates in other countries to build an unstoppable organization for good. For this work, which expanded the Isagenix movement worldwide, Gabby earned the Founder's Award—the first time it was awarded to someone outside North America. During her acceptance presentation, a native Maori man performed a traditional *haka* dance to honor Gabby's work on behalf of New Zealand's indigenous people.

Today, Gabby is still living her dream of helping others—plus so much more. Her parents hired someone else to run their thriving farm while they enjoy retirement beachside near Gabby. Countless working Kiwi's have returned to their homeland on the strength of their Isagenix earnings. And Gabby has helped change the health of thousands of families around the world. Plus, in the ultimate achievement of her "dream life" written down six years ago, Gabby met her soul mate Shayne and, together, they are expecting their first baby.

Single-handedly, Gabby Deane has not only proven to native New Zealanders that good health and a good income are possible, she has also overcome the cultural bias against "being successful" that has influenced local communities for decades.

"Isagenix is a way to live a life with no handicaps," Gabby says. "If you have poor health, a negative mindset, a poor bank account—you have handicaps to living the life you want."

---

*"Your playing small does not
serve the world."*

—MARIANNE WILLIAMSON
Bestselling author of A Return to Love

ONLY YOU CAN CREATE YOUR
OWN MOMENTUM

Day by day, the stories inspired me to keep on moving forward and bring even more people into the Isagenix family. I thought, *Impacting people's lives—their well-being, lifestyle, family, finances—this is my sole motivation…for everything!*

While I think I had known it all along—though I'd seen glimpses of it happening over the years in my own career—I soon realized the truth behind one of life's greatest lessons: *in the beginning, you create your own momentum.* But when you're determined—and especially when your goal is for the greater good—before long the resources, people and opportunities you need to get to the next level will show up to help you build your vision.

And that is exactly what happened at Isagenix.

One dynamic couple saw this momentum and joined us: Herb and Patty Cepada. While they had extensive experience in network marketing, they were blown away by our products and especially the Isagenix comp plan. They quickly built an organization through in-home presentations—talking to everyone they knew.

Women network-marketing leaders started to come to our company— looking for more support, a better diversified product mix, the potential to earn more money, and—most importantly—the ability to impact more lives.

Leaders from established network-marketing companies in business for decades—companies that were household names—started to join for the exact same reason. But they also wanted to be aligned with a company culture they could be proud of. They were looking for something that could be not just a legacy for their families, but also a company where their families could work together.

I love that about Isagenix. It's a legacy that will continue.

Leaders from the party-plan industry also started to join. They saw how quickly they could move to the top with our compensation plan. But even more importantly, they got excited about the potential of being paid on their entire team.

As a company, we were building a reputation for being loyal and supportive of our associates—a culture that attracted seasoned professionals to Isagenix, as well as offering a proven pathway for those with no prior experience. We care about our people and love them. We want them to have it all.

Additionally, as the company began to really hit its stride, we looked for top management talent who would help take us to the next level. Little did I know that one single decision would teach me completely new life lessons—and I've relied on them ever since. For one thing, Jim and I both learned to let go of the steering wheel a bit in order to focus on the bigger picture: growing our associates as people, creating new products, expanding into other countries—and honestly?—spending more time taking care of ourselves.

A new CEO helped us build an infrastructure and organization to support new growth. Suddenly, we now had the right people in the right seats on the bus. We had new financial capacity that would handle a rapid increase in sales and (more importantly) protect us from the cash-flow problems that commonly hit other companies in this industry.

With things being managed well at head office, Jim and I were able to travel more, not only around North America, but into our international markets, too. In the past, it had been rare for Jim to travel with me. But now, I love the fact that he could go with me to share our vision in other markets and train our people on the wonderful benefits of the network marketing profession. We were able to pour hope and belief into our field and help them achieve their goals.

Closer to home, one of our dreams was beginning to take shape. Our son Erik, who was now in college and intent on becoming a professional golfer, saw the benefits of having a supplemental income and the time freedom that our associate business opportunity could provide. While it was always our hope that he would one day join us in running the business, we never wanted to pressure him. We did, however, let him know that if he ever did choose to join us that it would be invaluable to know how to build and support a field organization. So he began as an associate and began building a team of athletes and Millennials seeking similar goals. After graduating from Business School, he decided to join us, starting at the bottom in our sales department. With his natural drive and determination, I thought deep down, *One day he'll make a huge impact.*

By 2013, our sales had really started to escalate. We added even more money to the Isagenix compensation plan, and it was becoming clear to everyone that Isagenix was the place to make a great income.

With internal growth that was off the charts—and interest from top leaders in countries around the world—the timing was right to turn Isagenix into a global brand. Our original vision for impacting people's lives—which I had dreamed of so many years before and had worked my entire career to achieve—was about to jump to hyperspeed.

What does it take to build something that has an impact beyond yourself? What can you do to be a visionary, not only imagining a bold new future for your own life and family, but also imagining an expansive future for countless other people, too?

Growing yourself as a person is the key to becoming a visionary. Gaining new experience, learning new skills, and working with others who've been there before you are just a few ways to grow. The following tips will give you more:

Find Out What's Possible, Then Dream Big

Today, too many people have given up on their dreams. What they want seems so unattainable, they stop believing it's even possible.

If you've lost touch with what you really want, it's time to start envisioning big things for yourself again. One exercise I like is to pull out eight pieces of paper and label each one at the top with the major areas of your life: finances; career or work; possessions; health; relationships; free time; personal growth; and contribution to your community. Perhaps you'd like to retire early with a net worth of $2 million. Write that down. Maybe you'd like to own a house at the beach or a vintage sports car...enjoy vibrant good health...work from home...meet your soul mate...start a charity...or travel the world. Whatever you want, write it down—whether or not you can afford it right now, or achieve it with your current skills. Write down your dreams.

Now ask yourself, *Are there people who buy these things and achieve these lifestyle standards? Are other people living the kind of life that I want to live? Regardless of how they did it, is it possible for me?*

Of course it is.

The key is to do your homework and find what *you need to do* to achieve the same thing. If you want to own an expensive sailboat for instance, have you researched what's involved in owning an investment of that caliber? For instance, do you know how much they cost? Once you acquire it, where would it be harbored? Do you need a special license or crew to pilot the boat? How much does maintenance cost?

Finding out what's possible—then researching the actions you need to take or the costs you have to cover—will help you establish some belief that your dreams are possible with enough money, time, knowledge, connections or other resources you can acquire. It will also help you set goals for achieving your dream, such as: *Research how to get a boating license in my state. Attend the Miami Boat Show in February. Research boat financing, leasing and rent-to-own. Schedule a week in July to charter the model I want.*

Research like this will help you discover what's possible, then add your own dreams to those possibilities. When you do find out what's possible, dream big and take action.

"Whatever the mind can conceive and believe,
the mind can achieve."

—NAPOLEON HILL
Bestselling author of Think and Grow Rich

Find a Role Model Who's Already Living Your Vision

Today, we live in a very advanced world. Technology, machines and automation let us do hundreds of things effortlessly that weren't even possible just a decade ago. What's more, everyday people are *easily* accomplishing things our grandparents only dreamed about 30-40 years ago. Whether it's owning a home, starting a business, traveling the world, winning an award or something else, there are more people than ever who have accomplished these goals—including many who've already accomplished *exactly what you want to do.*

In his book, *Unlimited Power,* Anthony Robbins says that, *Success leaves clues.* If there's something you want to accomplish, it's likely that somewhere—someone—has already done it *and documented the process.* It's only up to you to access this information, create a plan for duplicating their actions, then break down your plan into daily tasks that will help you reach your goal.

Spread Your Wings and Fly

You deserve an extraordinary life. But have you ever wondered how you would handle it if everything you wanted dropped into your lap today? Would you know how to manage your money, handle the fame or respond to the extra responsibilities? Would you have the experience or knowledge that your "perfect life" requires?

Of course not.

But the one thing you *can do* right now is to get ready for this expanded life. Get out there and get some experience—not only so you can work smarter to bring your vision to life, but also so you'll know exactly what to do when your goals begin to be achieved.

How do you get experience? Lean into it. Take small steps to build confidence. Learn by doing. Face your fears and be willing to step out of your comfort zone to grow yourself and others.

CHAPTER 3:

Be Willing to Ask

*"Asking is the beginning
of receiving."*

—JIM ROHN
Self-made millionaire and success philosopher

Every day, it seemed as though something triggered our expansion. We had new leaders emerging in new areas of the US and Canada. It was exciting!

But perhaps the biggest opportunity for growth required me and Jim, as well as our entire management team, to step up in a way we never saw coming. On Christmas Eve 2004, our legal team told us that John Anderson—our business partner and the brilliant formulator behind the Isagenix products—was suffering from kidney failure. In order to focus on his health, he needed to sell his majority interest in the company immediately.

This was a defining moment for us. Should we do what was needed to acquire John's majority stake—or run the risk of letting it go to an investor we didn't even know? There was only one possible answer: Jim and I decided to put everything on the line for this company we had built, and for the nearly 30,000 customers and associates who were relying on us. Yet with that one decision, our entire life was about to change.

With the help of our good friend, Jim Pierce, we quickly arranged to bring in a small private-equity group to provide the necessary cash, while we also began an aggressive management restructuring. Between the three of us—me, my husband and Jim Pierce—we stepped into executive roles, while the two Jim's began to build a world-class management team to support massive growth.

It worked.

Over the next year, we doubled the revenue of the company from $50 million to $100 million, and within two short years, we were able to pay back the private-equity firm all the cash they'd put up. That same year, we expanded into Hong Kong, Australia and New Zealand, then Taiwan and shortly thereafter, Mexico. This was the beginning of our global expansion.

United Kingdom quickly followed, then Ireland and Netherlands. Later, we expanded into Belgium, Spain and South Korea. Nothing was stopping the Isagenix train.

Our vision was being realized.

"Everything you want is out there
waiting for you to ask."

—JULES RENARD
French author and philosopher

WHAT DO <u>YOU</u> NEED TO ASK FOR?

Jack Canfield, who I mentioned earlier was a frequent speaker at our national conventions in the early years, wrote a terrific book, *The Success Principles: How to Get From Where You Are to Where You Want to Be.* In addition to teaching me so much about leading a high-growth company, Jack's book also taught me a lot about the art of asking.

While several of his asking strategies have been powerful lessons for me, three stand out in my mind as "most recommended" for Isagenix associates who want to build it big in the network-marketing business:

Ask as if you expect to get a "yes." Keeping a positive expectation is so important. When you ask from a place that it's a done deal, you've already got what you wanted, and that person you were pursuing has already decided, you show up with so much more confidence. *Of course what I have to offer is the solution they need,* you tell yourself. *I have the answer that will change their life and lifestyle.* As Jack recommends, always assume a successful outcome; don't ever assume against yourself.

Be clear and specific. Vague requests produce vague results. When you ask for something—a phone appointment or attendance at an event, for instance—be specific about what will take place and why you think it's important for them to show up. This also applies when "asking for the sale": clearly state the level, the product pack, the deadline and other specifics. Remember that you're the expert here; they're looking to you to specify the best way to start.

Ask repeatedly. Persistence pays off. What people say "no" to today, they might desperately need three months from now. What's not very persuasive today might be the exact thing they need next year to boost their income, get healthy, lose weight, help them get out of a bad relationship, or give them a new career. Life is like a moving parade: people's lives are always changing and evolving. Keep in touch. Keep asking. While the timing may not be right today, next month or next year *it just may be.*

"WHEN YOU HAVE THE PATH TO GETTING PAID, YOU HAVE TO SHARE THAT WITH PEOPLE"

One person who is terrific at "The Art of The Ask" is Trudy Maples. Trudy is one of those ladies you immediately fall in love with. Her enthusiasm is infectious and her drive to impact others draws you toward her. I remember being immediately impressed by her work ethic—and even today, it's something I really respect about her.

Trudy was already #2 in sales with another company when her sister introduced her to Isagenix. Growing up, Trudy had dreamed of someday making a great income. As a sixth-grader, she already knew she wanted her own business, "and a cleaning lady to clean my house every week," she recalls.

Trudy had been in network marketing since she was 26 years old. She worked hard and did her homework. She even started a catering business and ran a cooking school as another income stream. Her husband Nathan, a student pastor at the time, brought in additional income.

But after 19 years with the other company, the most Trudy ever made was $65,000 a year.

"When my sister first shared Isagenix with me," Trudy remembers, "she talked enthusiastically about the products. But as a caterer, the thought of trading shakes for gourmet dinners made me skeptical."

Eventually, however, Trudy's sister shared the Isagenix compensation plan, and after that, Trudy was all in.

"I'd been working so hard for 19 years," Trudy said. The Isagenix comp plan was a revelation.

Just the fact that she could earn on her entire team was enough to convince Trudy. And holdover volume? From a legacy company? She immediately knew what she could do.

Still, it took Trudy 15 months to finish up her commitments for cooking classes and catering jobs before she could jump in and start building an Isagenix business. Once she got started, however, her remarkable work ethic paid off: in her first year, she already found herself in the top 1% of all income earners. This is not "the norm," but Trudy poured her heart and soul into this business. What I love about her most is her ability to pour belief into people—something that helped her achieve this amazing level of income so quickly.

Using her catering background, she held tasting parties for Isagenix products before that was common. She became a walking billboard for the Isagenix product line—losing 35 pounds and looking fabulous. Never much into Facebook, Trudy started talking up the comp plan online and "created major FOMO about her physical and financial transformation on social media," she said.

She was named Leader of the Year in her very first year, and went on to earn a top spot in every incentive that first year, too. Just recently, she and Nathan were named Isagenix Couple of the Year.

Finding people with heart and hustle—who love to serve and who are self-motivated and confident—has been Trudy's formula for success.

"You can teach skills all day, but you can't teach the will to succeed," Trudy says. "I can teach the skill, but they have to have the will."

This priority shows in her organization, which focuses on building legacy teams for families—her most important priority. Past experience has taught her that people will do whatever it takes to accomplish that major goal. But more important than just a paycheck, it's truly about transforming people's lives.

"When you have the path to getting paid, you HAVE to share that with people," says Trudy as she reminisces about the new associates who said yes to the Isagenix opportunity in the midst of family, career and financial trouble. "It's transformational."

Today, she's a consistent enroller on her own—she never asks her team to do something that she won't do. Plus, she always leads the conversation with the road map to Crystal Executive level and the income that comes along the way.

What's more, Trudy and her husband believe that *who you are is who you attract.* They focus on being a terrific married couple *first* with a positive mindset for whom personal development is a top priority.

---

*"You must go after the things you desire
like your life depends on it, because guess what?
Your life does depend on it.
The life you truly want to live does."*

—JEN SINCERO
New York Times *bestselling author of* You Are a Badass

CREATE A VISION BOARD TO HELP YOU STAY FOCUSED ON YOUR "WHY"

A *vision board* is a colorful collage of images that you display somewhere you pass by frequently—in your home or office—to remind you of the outcomes you're striving for. When you see pictures of your dream home, a luxury trip to Paris, your mortgage marked "paid," your kids in top colleges, plus pictures, words and other reminders of your compelling future, you'll stay more focused and on-task.

Trudy Maples holds a "dream session" with people, then helps them create digital vision boards they can turn into a screen saver or smartphone wallpaper—anywhere they'll see it frequently and be reminded why they're working hard. Trudy calls her process "vision casting," an empowering and emotional session when people not only express their heartfelt dreams—perhaps for the first time in years—but also begin believing their dreams are possible again. Early in her career, Trudy held team-building parties to clip magazine photos and create physical vision boards. Now her team uses Pic•Collage, an app* that not only assembles your digital photos and screenshots into a collage that can be used almost anywhere, it also lets you update photos and cross things off as you accomplish them.

ASK LIKE SOMEONE'S LIFE DEPENDS ON IT

One lesson I've learned over the years is so powerful when it comes to asking: *If you have a way to improve people's lives, you have no right to keep that information to yourself.*

As our products were changing people's wellbeing, a new trend began to emerge that I had never seen before on this scale: women were "retiring" their husbands at a record rate. And whether these men joined their wives in the family's Isagenix business or pursued something different—investing, ministry, teaching or entrepreneurship, for example—the money these women were earning had the power to improve people's livelihoods and lifestyles.

One story I want to share is about a woman who is a real beauty. While her early goal with Isagenix was to help her family get out of massive debt, her "why" suddenly changed, and this new burning desire—as we'll learn—helped

---

* *Visit* pic-collage.com.

her quickly move to the top of the company. She now leads with grace and commitment to help other families achieve their dreams.

For three years, Laura Stevens had watched her friend build an Isagenix business, help lots of people, and eventually retire her husband from the corporate rat-race. It was a charmed life. And a far cry from the one that Laura and her husband John were living.

An artillery officer in the United States Marines, John was scheduled to deploy to Iraq any day, leaving Laura to manage their young family, their household, and unfortunately, their debts. Through some bad financial decisions and multiple student loans, they'd racked up $80,000 in obligations—debt that Laura had worked hard to pay down with side hustles over the years. Though she knew about Isagenix and saw her friend experience success, Laura didn't trust the network-marketing industry. Still, as John went off to the frontlines to fight ISIS, Laura wondered what more she could do.

Most military wives who've lived through multiple deployments will tell you that families who stay behind have two choices: sadness and resignation —or using that time apart to focus on something that will uplevel the family's future. Laura decided to pour every ounce of her energy into building an Isagenix business. Her faith told her that God had put this opportunity in their lives to bless their family. John had six years left before he could retire from the military. And Laura was fired up to create the kind of financial stability that would give him choices and maybe even the ability to retire early and pursue an encore career.

Laura's energy and focus helped her start quickly and see early success. She told her friends how important this was for her family, and asked them to do one of three things: be supportive and excited for her; pass along the names of anyone she could help who needed extra income; or join her in the Isagenix opportunity. With every promotion the company offered, Laura saw her husband and kids behind each goal—a mindset that helped her work harder, be bolder, and take action more consistently, knowing it would change their lives.

Soon, her efforts began to pay off.

Then, on February 13, 2015 while Laura sat in the Denver airport awaiting her flight to an Isagenix Super Saturday event, the terminal's television screens began to broadcast a breaking news report: ISIS fighters were attacking al-Asad Airbase where John was deployed. As she watched with growing panic—knowing John couldn't even text her that he was okay—Laura's determination to change their future intensified.

Within a year, she had achieved the kind of income and built the kind of organization she needed to bring John home for good. Through Laura's hard work—and her courage to ask friends to help her business grow—she had paid off their debt and could finally afford to support their family on her Isagenix income alone. When in June 2016, the Pentagon announced they were downsizing the military, John jumped at the chance for early retirement and joined Laura in further growing the family's Isagenix business.

John Stevens' life depended on Laura asking repeatedly and with confidence. What could you accomplish with your own Isagenix business by getting better at talking to people?

ASK WITH A BIG VISION IN MIND

Though we had opened Australia with big plans, we also realized that it simply takes time for leaders to emerge in new markets. To help that process during the first few years, Jim and I—along with our son Erik who was taking on more and more responsibility at Isagenix—traveled to Sydney, Melbourne, Brisbane, Perth, Gold Coast, and other cities in Australia to train emerging leaders and help grow teams locally. By then, Erik had begun to see a future trend emerge.

"Mom, everyone in your company is old. You need more young people in Isagenix," he'd said during his first few months at the company.

His vision was to ignite Millennials in every corner of the world to look at network marketing—and Isagenix, specifically—as a bona fide profession and alternative to building wealth. He wanted to fill Isagenix with exciting ideas and younger people—"digital natives" who would use the best of technology, social media, and global thinking to build their teams. He wanted to emphasize ways that younger people could contribute to their communities, but also achieve freedom—time freedom, financial freedom, freedom from economic downturns and the other twists and turns of life—then bring that same freedom to others.

Handing me a paper napkin with a rough drawing on it, Erik pointed to the logo he'd created for this big new vision: *START,* it read.

START

Through the simple act of Erik asking, *What can we do differently as a company? Who else do we need to reach? Who else out there needs this opportunity?,* a new level of excitement and energy was expanding Isagenix around the world, with Millennials becoming one of the fastest-growing groups in the company.

THE "START" VISION IS BORN

Start Your Life, the movement's vision statement begins. *Our vision is to ignite all young people to own their lives physically and financially, and—through our contributions—create freedom and a lasting legacy.*

If there was one thing Erik knew for certain, it's that Jim and I wanted to create a legacy company that would support our associates and their families for generations to come.

"The thing that I feel responsible for, in my soul," Erik said, "is carrying the torch of this great company into the future."

Knowing that *young people* represent the next generation of leaders, Erik began the START movement to seek out, inspire and mobilize Millennials and young professionals who could insure this legacy for decades. Day by day, Erik and a handful of early START leaders began to ignite this younger demographic—age 18 to 35—to look at Isagenix as a career, a community, and their passion. New associates began to emerge from every country in our network, with enormous heart, talent, interests—and networks of their own. To these early leaders, Isagenix was a way to create not just an enviable income, but also *anything else* they wanted in their life: the ideal body, the ideal tribe, the lifestyle of their dreams, a way to help others, and enough money to start making plans for their future.

Within months, the movement took off.

Over 60,000 people plugged into the START community via its Facebook hub in just the first few years. And, as social proof has grown—as young, successful Isagenix entrepreneurs have shared their stories online—thousands of *other* young people have joined Isagenix and created a potent new culture in the company.

"Community is key," says Erik. "The idea that you're not alone in the pursuit of good health, or in building your own business, is very powerful. But so is the idea that you are becoming part of something bigger than yourself."

For instance, Erik suggested that START events include unique elements that would appeal to young people, but that fit their lifestyle, too. Most include some form of giving back—whether it's helping a local shelter with a work day or planting trees in a nearby town. And all include face-to-face time where social interaction is key.

"We're the most technically connected generation, but we've never been more disconnected," he reflects. "Everyone's face-planted to their phone. So successful young Isagenix leaders are getting together face-to-face—either online or in person—to make human connections and share fun activities."

But young people also want to create change in the world. They thrive in a group where they're empowered to impact both themselves *and* others for the better. So perhaps the most important product that Isagenix offers this generation—in addition to physical health and financial health—is a sense of community.

"It's always good business to position a company around trends that aren't going away," says Erik. "And one trend that's not going away is people wanting to get together in person. Most people are starving for human interaction. We talk a lot about physical health and financial health, but people are yearning for *social health* more than anything."

Part of that healthy social interaction is contribution: giving back.

Erik was frustrated by companies that lure young people with flashy objects—which appeals to them only in the short term. Instead, he wanted to create a movement of extraordinary people whose impact would be sustainable over time.

"We've been clear with START that Isagenix is not really about material possessions," Erik explains.

It's about owning your life physically and financially, but most importantly, it's about inspiring you to recirculate some of that money, time, energy and resources to improve the world.

"I want START to grow young people who you could drop anywhere in the world, and—just because of how they show up—that community begins to change," he continued. "Drop them anywhere and good things will happen."

While this "ripple effect" is a goal that lots of companies talk about, few actually bring it into being. By emphasizing this key characteristic in the START movement, the appeal of Isagenix to Millennials is not only sustainable, but it's also what attracts them in the first place. Young people are joining Isagenix for all the right reasons.

"The quality of people we've attracted is amazing," Erik concludes. "And, as we all know, we're a product of the people we surround ourselves with."

By his own admission, the START community has made Erik a better company leader, a better husband and a better dad. In fact, his #1 goal for START from the beginning has been to create a community that empowers young people to pursue their goals, stay healthy, create extra income, and change their situation in life for the better.

What can I say...I am so proud of Erik. He inspires me every day.

"If you throw a pebble into the water on one side of the ocean, it can create a tidal wave on the other side."

—VICTOR WEBSTER

Actor

ASK PEOPLE WHO ALIGN WITH YOUR VISION

As the Australian market began to really grow, we kept hearing about a lady, Peta Kelly, who other associates Down Under called "Earth Angel." She was from Perth and was making huge strides in building her team. Not only did she align 100% with Erik's vision for the START movement, she took it to the next level—enrolling hundreds of Millennials, giving them a path to success, and growing them as dynamic new leaders. She started a series of events in Australia called Wellness Wednesdays, and the younger generation poured into the company.

Today, Peta and Erik are married, and Jim and I have two beautiful grandchildren. Peta is one of those women who makes a huge impact on you once you see inside her soul. She is a thought leader that inspires everyone around her to do more, want more, and live a life of their own design.

Studying for her Ph.D. in Exercise and Health Science on a $500-a-week government scholarship, 24-year-old Peta Kelly thought her future lay in research. She wanted to pursue a career that would let her be of service to mankind. However, Peta always felt intuitively that there was something wrong with the "default" life proposed to us by society. It didn't make sense to her that people worked at jobs they hate—just so they could enjoy their lives just a little. She knew there was a different way, but wasn't yet clear on how.

She always knew there was more, but didn't focus on becoming wealthy from her science work, nor did she concentrate on following her dream of traveling the world. For six years, she focused on hardcore studying. She even had a research paper published in an international journal. She thought that, to live her ultimate dream, she had to first chase the success that came from exchanging time for money.

But one day, her heart pulled her inescapably in the direction of her dream. Almost without thinking, she travelled around Southeast Asia with her friend Jo. It was Jo who introduced Peta to Isagenix.

Today, at the age of 31, Peta travels the world, gives to the causes she cares about, and spends her time without restrictions—all while continuing to earn a sizable residual income from Isagenix.* Not only that, but Peta has also written three books, created new companies, held her own events—and has used Isagenix as a way to follow her other passions and callings. Most importantly, she is Mum to two beautiful kids and intentionally lives in a very alternative way—travelling the world as a family and being a present mum, as well as creating the things that call her.

She didn't accomplish that overnight, however. Along the way, Peta struggled and faced moments when she wanted to stop. She knew that Isagenix products provided wellness of the body, but what she eventually realized is that *wellness* is actually the well-being of your whole life.

Unless you have *financial wellness* too, Peta realized, you're not "well" at all —a realization that, coming off of six years doing research at one of the top universities in the world, hit her hard. Still, she wondered. If financial wellness had changed her life for the better, what else could it do?

---

* *Results not typical.*

Instantly, she thought of her mum—a single mother of four—who had provided everything for them: the best schools, elite sports, the perfect childhood. In her heart, Peta wanted to provide for her mother in return. She always knew she would, she just wasn't sure how.

At Isagenix's annual Celebration event that year, Peta's heart lit up with a goal to pay off her mum's mortgage and help her retire from her 40-year teaching job.

Changing her mum's life became Peta's "why."

She became an intense worker—a "sponsor monster"—working early in the morning until late at night. She was on fire. Yet six months later, she was still making just $500 a week. Not only that, but Peta's friends didn't get it: she'd left her Ph.D. to do this, yet she wasn't making any real money and her dream of retiring her mum seemed further away than ever.

Peta was close to stopping altogether and finding a different path to help fund her vision, until she realized: it's not enough to have a light on in your heart. You need *immediate why's*—short-term goals that will keep you focused and become fuel for your fire.

So what was the short-term goal that lit up Peta's motivation?

Her brother Ben—stuck in a job he hated and faced with crippling debt —had lost the carefree smile Peta remembered from their childhood. When the next Isagenix event came around, she dragged him there—and within three months, he was able to walk away from his job to focus on building alongside Peta full time.*

Peta had a burning excitement within her to see other young people living the same life she had: time freedom, supportive friends, a common goal with others who were successful. She wanted to take young people under her wing and say, "You can have whatever you want. Let's do this."

She wanted to help them walk away from jobs they hated...travel to exotic places at a moment's notice...and passionately pursue whatever lifelong

---

* *Results not typical.*

dream they'd had. Transforming *their* lives became her new calling—a "pull" that she could be passionate about.

"If you are working on something that you really care about, you don't have to be pushed. The vision pulls you."

—STEVE JOBS
Founder of Apple Inc.

Peta was successful and wanted to share that with others her age. But, unfortunately, in Perth—where she was living—Australians are known for a limiting belief called *Tall Poppy Syndrome.* If you do well—if you grow and achieve higher than others—people try to cut you down.

Undeterred, Peta chose instead to live the Isagenix success story out loud, making no apologies for helping people. She started celebrating on Facebook everything that young Isagenix associates were doing. Even when longtime friends bullied her on social media for reaching so high—which was heartbreaking—she kept going, pulled by the vision of her dream for others.

She began to ask two questions of the people on her team: (1) what excites you?, and (2) what excites you *now?*

Listening to their answers, Peta realized that the team she was building was more than just a collaboration of people in the same business. They were kindred spirits drawn to the same things and striving to live the same way Peta was: with unstoppable passion.

Focusing on her "why" helped Peta stay focused and motivated. Within two years, Peta and her brother Ben—who'd joined her in Isagenix—were able to retire their mother from her 40-year teaching career.

Asking others about their why made Peta's *own why* come true.

"Passion is energy. Feel the power that comes
from focusing on what excites you."

—OPRAH WINFREY
Billionaire talk-show host, actress, author and philanthropist

FEED THE FLAME WITHIN YOU

Once we saw the positive effect that Peta's training was having on teams everywhere, we asked her to present at the national convention on determining your "why." Like so many things that are simple, but which can profoundly impact growth, Peta's presentation changed the game for Isagenix, and as you'll see in these tips, her principles are easy to apply.

Ask What Excites You Now

Have you ever thought about what makes you happy? Or what makes you daydream?

What gives you joy just thinking about it? What fires you up every day to achieve your goals and your vision?

That flame, that pull, that passion... that's your "why."

When we look at successful companies and teams to explain what they do to succeed, a pattern emerges: what, how and why.

But instead of starting with *what they'll do* to achieve success—or *how they'll achieve it*—Peta Kelly explains that top teams start with the question: *why are we doing this?* They function from a place of inspiration—when an idea gets a hold of you and you're pulled. You feel called.

Having a "why" just makes life easier. You'll always know where you're headed. You'll always know what to do. You'll wake up each day in a state of joyful expectation, with energy and excitement for your goals. In fact, our emotions are actually a clue to what's pulling us.

So what gives *you* the most joy, happiness, and passion?

Remember, too, that you can have both a short-term *why* (like getting out of debt) and a future *why* (like retiring your parents to a life of leisure).

We all need something that will give us a little reward in the present while we're working on those faraway goals. So ask yourself what excites you *now*—immediately—and what will keep you focused and motivated over the next 90 days' time.

"Let yourself be silently drawn by the strange pull of what you really love. It will not lead you astray."

—RUMI

13th Century Persian poet, scholar, and theologian

Ask What Excites Your Team

Network marketing is not all about what you want. It's also about finding out what your people need. Ask your team members what excites them. Show them how to achieve their dreams and goals through this amazing vehicle. You can turn the lights on for thousands of others whose success and passion will keep *you* motivated. You can also motivate others to create a "why" by helping them dream again. So many people give up on their dreams because they do not have the right vehicle to achieve success.

They haven't experienced the possibilities available to dream beyond their own limited view of the world.

Asking what excites her team prompted Peta Kelly to start meetings she called "Wellness Wednesdays" to excite her team about their own personal why. Eventually, as leaders emerged, Peta collaborated with them to speak at these meetings without her guidance or oversight.

The motivational and inspirational tone of the meetings attracted people to the team—and to the team's collective vision. Through Wellness Wednesdays, people who cared about the same thing could support and train each other.

SIMPLE STEPS TO START ASKING

Every successful story starts with asking someone to join you in your own passionate pursuit. And when it comes to asking someone to join your Isagenix team, here are several ideas to help people see the possibilities for their future:

Find out what's missing in their life. Most people would like to do better. They feel that something is missing—financial security, good health, low-stress lifestyle, supportive relationships…whatever it is, find out. Ask as any friend would do—with genuine interest and concern. You'd be surprised at the answers. Even people who seem to have everything yearn for more, even if it's something productive, fun or rewarding to do with their day.

Ask, too, about their personal health goals. Are they getting the best nutrition, maintaining their ideal weight, getting enough exercise and drinking plenty of water? Do they have long-standing health conditions that concern them? Would they like to lose weight, have more energy, have more mental clarity throughout the day, and glow with good health?

Find out why they want to achieve these health goals. Would being slimmer and healthier give them more confidence in their career or personal life? Do they want to be healthy in order to live longer? Do they want the energy and vitality that comes from maintaining their ideal weight and getting better nutrition?

After asking about their health goals, find out what they would like to accomplish financially. Do they want to eliminate debt, send their children to the best schools, or go on that dream vacation? Would they like to help their parents live a better quality of life? Is there something unique they've always wanted to do that could be accomplished with additional income such as owning a vacation home, donating to a charity, retiring early, helping their spouse escape the corporate rat-race, or moving to another city?

One question that really helps people think about their financial goals is this one: *Has there been a time lately when you had to say "no" to your children or spouse because you didn't have the money to say "yes"?* This question not only makes the conversation personal, it also helps people realize they do have gaps in their financial life. Finally, be sure to ask how much money they would need *on a monthly basis* to achieve their ideal life.

Most importantly, cast the vision about what's possible with Isagenix. The reality is that our world is changing, and Isagenix can help people change with the times. Today, people want to work differently: they want flexibility and time freedom. They're also tired of helping company owners achieve their dreams and goals—they want to achieve *their own dreams* instead. Isagenix is the perfect vehicle for doing that.

Unfortunately, most people don't really understand how network marketing helps everyone win. When you identify someone in your network who's willing to work hard to build a business, it's in *your* best interest to help them achieve success. In fact, network marketing is the only business model where you climb the ladder when you help *your people* succeed. Compare that to the corporate world where many people succeed at the expense of someone else.

Succeeding in network marketing is as simple as building a network of people who buy and consume the best products in the world. You receive commission on the sale of products purchased by people in your network.

Not only that, but the network marketing industry accounted for around $190 billion in business in 2019 (worldwide), so there's enough room for everyone to do well financially if they're willing to make a consistent effort. Plus, the Health and Wellness segment *dominates* the greater network marketing industry! Isagenix—with its recognized wellness products—is a company that has the highest values and is here to stay so you can create a legacy of future earnings for your family.

Ask them to check out the New Associate tools. When you send a welcome email to a new associate you've enrolled, be sure to ask them to check out the informative videos at *IsaMovie.com*—filled with information about the products and the Isagenix wealth-creation opportunity. Ask them to read more about the products at *IsaProduct.com*. And, finally, ask them to review what other successful associates have learned at *IsagenixBusiness.com*.

Ask them to join you on a 3-way call. It's long been known that one of the criteria humans use to make a buying decision is *social proof:* what other people have experienced with a product, company, or purchase. In this age of social media and online reviews, social proof is even more impactful, which is why one of your very first "asks" should be an invitation to a 3-way call with you and someone in leadership on your team.

Complete the New Associate Interview. Asking these questions will help you learn more about them as a person, plus it goes a long way toward creating a solid relationship.*

ULTIMATELY, ASKING TAKES COURAGE

As Isagenix grew and expanded, we discovered fearless and motivated people like Peta and her team in unexpected places. These were "people with a why" who had become determined to succeed.

Of course, asking others to join the Isagenix movement took courage. And in the next chapter, I'll reveal how *unstoppable courage* is available to everyone.

---

* *Find the document at* https://www.isagenix.com/-/media/coaching-opportunity/new-associate-customer-interview/associate/id-en-new-associate-interview

CHAPTER 4:

Have Courage

"We must look for ways to be an active force in our own lives. We must take charge of our own destinies, design a life of substance, and truly begin to live our dreams."

—LES BROWN
Bestselling author, motivational speaker, and talk-show host

As the company grew and new opportunities for growth poured in, I thought often in those days of what my dad had taught me.

Every night before I went to bed, my dad would come to say goodnight. He would pour his wisdom into my ears.

"You can do anything you put your heart and soul into," he would say. "You're the most determined person I know. Someday your time will come to shine."

Have courage. Never give up.

In grammar school and high school I excelled in sports—breaking records for track and swimming. Winning at sports taught me the power of focus, the value of teamwork, and how to look for the lessons whenever I won or lost. It also taught me the importance of practice, practice, practice.

But school also taught me something more.

In those days, I went to a private Catholic, all-girls school and struggled academically. I was constantly chastised by the nuns, who scolded, "Why can't you be focused like Mary Beth or Cindy?"

The reprimands affected me internally, but my dad continued to pour greatness into me. When I graduated, the principal told me, as she handed me my diploma, *You will never make it . . .* words, she said, that would make me tougher.

Going off to college was a relief. In fact, once I was free from the bullying, I excelled and graduated first in my class. While the harsh words of the principal indeed made me tougher, my dad's loving encouragement spoke even louder: "You are the best. You never give up. Keep fighting. Keep going until you win."

RESILIENCE MEANS HAVING THE COURAGE
TO KEEP GOING UNTIL YOU WIN

Starting classes in dental hygiene school at Foothill College in the San Francisco Bay Area was exciting. I had recovered from my cancer scare by my 19th birthday, and married my high school sweetheart that same year.

The future seemed so bright. In fact, the world seemed open to anything I wanted to achieve.

But making the two-hour commute each way to school—as a newlywed and with extra studies after I got home—took its toll on me. I nearly had a breakdown. But, once again, my father poured his wisdom and belief into me: "You can do this, Kathy. You have to be able to support yourself," he said. "Never count on anyone else to support you."

It gave me the resilience to keep going and graduate first in my class.

But little did I know how important that advice would be.

While my professional future seemed unlimited in those days, the bloom began to fade in my marriage. As my career soared, the man I had chosen as my husband—a demon who I'd entrusted with my love and my future—became mentally and physically abusive. For years, he had put me down and fought everything I did. He told me I was stupid, ugly—that no one else would want me. I almost began to believe his bullying words. Then the physical violence began. I was constantly in fear.

When I almost lost my life to his anger and the horrors of his abuse, I finally got the courage to leave.

HAVE THE COURAGE TO LET
A NEW LIFE BLOSSOM

Within weeks, I started to work on myself—hoping to recapture the sense of self-worth and achievement I'd grown up with. I found a great counselor who helped me realize so many things about myself.

"There are great men out there," she said. "But you really need to choose wisely. You need a man who will let you be you."

As my confidence began to emerge, I threw myself into my work. I started the first dental-hygiene center in California—where I actually had a dentist working for *me*. Once again, my father—a dentist himself *and* a self-made entrepreneur—encouraged me to think outside the box. The center became a huge success, giving me more flexibility and a larger income.

At 27 years old, I was having the time of my life.

I traveled, explored and discovered new things. I had the freedom to learn and grow. Finally, it felt as if my new life was beginning. And I was having fun. But more than that, I was happy.

When a friend introduced me to Jim at a Monday Night Football game, I was instantly attracted, but reluctant, too. I didn't want to jump into another relationship when I was enjoying my freedom to discover and grow. The great thing was that Jim was so busy with his own career, we could only see each other once a week. This gave me time to learn what I really needed in a relationship: respect, trust, communication, romance, and adventure. But what I really needed was the freedom to become myself. I needed someone who would let me complete my journey of self-discovery, and who would support me in my dreams and goals.

Someone who, together, could create new dreams and goals with me.

When Jim said, "Let's create a beautiful life together. I want to grow old with you," I knew he truly loved me. We married soon afterward, and it's been the best decision of my life.

HAVE THE COURAGE TO GROW TOGETHER

Jim and I started working together as business partners *28 years ago*. At first, it was a little clumsy. It took time to figure it out.

"What are your strengths? What are mine?" we'd asked each other. "What do you love to do, and how can we work together?"

We would constantly hone and refine our approach. Plus, in the early days, we also had to manage our schedules so that we could give Erik the love and support he needed to grow. I learned that setting goals together—then supporting each other as you pursue them—is just one of the keys to a solid relationship. Communication is another. You either grow together or you grow apart.

After 36 years of marriage, Jim and I have learned a lot about how to make our marriage continue to thrive: always remember to start your day with gratitude for your spouse. Tell them how much you love them, and how grateful you are for each other. It will make a huge difference—both in your marriage and in your life.

"At the root of every successful marriage is a strong partnership."

—CARSON DALY

Host of NBC's The Voice *television show*

HAVE THE COURAGE TO TRY A NEW PATH

One of the most life-changing (and courageous) things you can do for your future is to ask yourself, *What's not working in my life? What if I made different choices or tried something new?*

For instance, do you stay in that job you hate because it pays the bills? Do you stay in that toxic relationship because being on your own is scary? Do you tolerate your lack of energy, excess weight, or annoying health condition because doing something about it requires making tough choices? Do you suffer financially because of student loans or credit card debts that are so high, you wonder if they can ever be repaid?

Resilient people experience these life situations, too. But one of the hallmarks of these take-charge types is that they respond *differently*. They recognize bad situations for what they are. They face facts straight on. They move from denial to a determination to change their circumstances. And they rarely stay in circumstances that are stressful, demoralizing or unproductive. Instead, they take action to raise their standards and make things happen for themselves—and for the people they work with, the environment they live in, and the activities in their life.

They ask themselves instead: *What would my ideal life look like? Where would my children go to school? What neighborhood would we live in? What charities do I want to contribute to? What is the life of my dreams?*

Of course, forging a new path—and creating a new way of living—isn't easy. But the reality is there are other ways to pay the bills, get healthy, live free from toxic relationships, create financial security, and live the good life.

GRADUALLY, SHE BEGAN TO SEE A NEW PATH

Remember Laura Stevens, the military wife from *Chapter Three?* One day, she called me, excited to share that one of her best friends had joined the business.

"Could you call and get to know her?" Laura asked, describing the unique passion of her friend, Dr. Lindsay Hoffbuhr.

When Lindsay and I met for lunch in Lake Tahoe, where she lives, I was blown away by her beauty—both inside and out. Lindsay is one of the those special people you meet, where you immediately you say to yourself, *This lady has it all*...beauty, brains, drive, compassion and a deep desire to help people not only with their health, but to live the lives of their dreams, too.

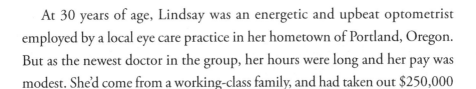

At 30 years of age, Lindsay was an energetic and upbeat optometrist employed by a local eye care practice in her hometown of Portland, Oregon. But as the newest doctor in the group, her hours were long and her pay was modest. She'd come from a working-class family, and had taken out $250,000

in student loans to pay for her education. A full six years into what she thought would be a well-paying healthcare career, Lindsay still had a staggering $225,000 to pay off over the loan's remaining 20-year term.

Her husband, Cory Hoffbuhr, was equally hardworking. A former U.S. Navy medic who'd left the military to become an anesthesiologist, Cory was in his first year of residency—earning next to nothing for long hours and a relentless schedule of surgeries.

Caring for patients, helping people, and working in the medical profession was something they both said they loved. But even Lindsay was beginning to wonder, *Where had it all gone wrong?*

Compounding her despair, she and Cory had started a family. Their two adorable daughters—aged 13 months and 3 years—got what little time and energy their hardworking parents had left. The couple's work-life balance was poor and their finances were even worse. Every extra dollar went to retiring the 20-year debt Lindsay had brought to their marriage.

Then one day, Lindsay's best friend from college introduced her to a line of nutritional products: Isagenix. Lindsay loved the way they made her feel and began to tell others about the energy boost and health benefits she was experiencing. When coworkers and friends wanted to order their own Isagenix products, Lindsay referred them to her college pal who—as any true friend would do—quietly signed them up under Lindsay's name. Within weeks, compensation checks for $100...$150...even $300 began to show up in the family's mailbox. Lindsay was astounded.

Gradually, she began to see a path to paying down her student loans—not in 20 years, as planned—but in 15 years...or maybe even 10.

I can lift the huge burden I've placed on my family, she thought.

Starting with just the spare time she had between patients—and working evening hours after the girls went to bed—Lindsay began to build her Isagenix business. She got to know the company, learned about the products and studied the compensation plan. To her delight, the compensation checks grew larger.

By the time her one-year anniversary as an Isagenix associate came around —just 365 days *to the day* after she'd tasted her first shake—Lindsay was receiving Isagenix checks that were *four times* what she was earning as an eye care professional. That was her "a-ha moment." She'd built an Isagenix income big enough to confidently submit her resignation at the optometry practice where she worked. She walked out of an exam room for the last time and walked straight into the arms of her two little girls—never once regretting her decision or worrying whether her family would survive financially. Not only had she already replaced her professional income, within two years she paid off the last of her $225,000 student loan debt, too.*

With one simple act of courage, Lindsay had created a new life for her family. Isagenix was the vehicle that changed everything for her.

Now, five years later, Lindsay has never once regretted leaving private practice. While she looks back on those years in the medical profession with fondness, she knows her family's life today is so much more abundant. It's far more flexible for her as a mom. And it's lots more fun.

But, most importantly, for a woman in the workplace, Lindsay now gets paid what she's worth. In fact, her pay is in direct correlation to how hard she works, her belief in herself and her consistency—something that is so difficult for women to find in the traditional workforce.

"It's challenging to stand up for yourself," Lindsay tells her team, "and ask for what you believe you are worth." Today, as part of her team training, she helps women understand that Isagenix is the vehicle for getting paid what you deserve.

Was it difficult to walk away from a medical career she'd dreamed of as a little girl and trained for her entire adult life? Was it difficult to answer the never-ending questions when friends asked, *Why would you walk away from years of education? Why would you give up your career?*

It was. Very difficult.

---

* *Results not typical.*

But, as Lindsay explains, while nothing can ever take away those first few years of job satisfaction or the doctorate degree that she is enormously proud of, she quickly realized that medical professionals aren't always paid what they're worth. And being a slave to a job at the risk of her family life was a surprising and unattractive part of the healthcare industry.

"Plus, nothing can change your heart like becoming a mom," she says.

Today, Lindsay is proof positive that *it is possible* to shift careers at any point in your life. What's more, she and Cory like to think that the other healthcare professionals who've joined them—the physician assistants, nurse practitioners, and operating room nurses—believe in the Isagenix opportunity because Lindsay paved the way. Because she was courageous in her own life, today other people can be courageous in theirs.

---

*"Doing more of what doesn't work won't
make it work any better."*

—CHARLES J. GIVENS
Author of Wealth Without Risk

ARE YOU SILENTLY STRUGGLING?

Whether your hardship is an unfulfilling job, overwhelming debt, an abusive relationship, a health battle or something else, struggling in silence will simply keep you in the same place you are now.

Having the courage to change your circumstances, on the other hand, is *the first step to creating a new life for yourself.*

In fact, the stories of people who had the courage to change is what drives me every day to do more, push harder, and never give up—so we can impact more lives both physically and financially.

- In the early days of Isagenix, I was introduced to a man who told me he was sick and tired of "being old, fat and broke." He had the guts to go for it, and now his family's life has been forever changed. They've bought five houses, so far, and continue to make an amazing income.*

- A single, female chiropractor who was in a desperate situation— with only $45 to her name, and who'd had to move back in with her mom—said, *Enough is enough*. She made the decision to get out of the rut of despair and is now one of our most successful women associates. She inspires chiropractors, gym owners, moms, and Millennials to join her community, and to go for their dreams and create a life of joy and fulfillment.

- Another woman I had the pleasure of meeting was desperate for change. Her weight was out of control, and she was deeply in debt. She made the decision to change her life, and sold her refrigerator to start her Isagenix business.

- In the beginning, a man who'd been educated in nutrition joined our vision. He traveled the western United States, speaking about his belief in our products. He had the brilliant idea of calling our system a *cleanse*. He and his wife blazed the trail for Isagenix in the first few years and are now living the life of their dreams.

- A young, single female bartender on the East Coast was burned out from working long hours. By the time her shift ended every night, it was 1:00 a.m. when she finally left the bar. She *knew* there was a better way. Now, through her Isagenix business, she's living the life of her dreams and earning more than most CEOs. She is passionate and enthusiastic to share her story with the world.

- A flight attendant from Canada was so burned out from being on long-haul flights, she couldn't stand it any longer. She jumped into Isagenix and has now been with us for 17 years building the life of her dreams.

---

* *Results not typical.*

These people learned that having courage is the first step to changing one's life (and lifestyle). Taking action—and working on playing a bigger game—is the second.

HAVE THE COURAGE TO PLAY A BIGGER GAME

Have you ever met someone who has the kind of glow and aura that draws you to them? An energy that is infectious and compassionate? Someone whose soul is driven to make a huge difference and help everyone? That is Abby O'Neil—a woman who gives and gives. She is unstoppable!

Twenty-two year old Abby O'Neil was smart, energetic and motivated. She'd gotten her business degree at the University of New Hampshire and, as a new mom herself, decided to pursue entrepreneurship in the childcare industry—both as a full-time nanny and running a staffing agency providing other nannies to local families. It seemed perfect, really. Abby could keep her baby daughter with her during the day and still run the business at night.

At first glance, she was successful. But a closer look revealed that Abby was exhausted. She loved her business, but never felt that her family came first. She didn't feel healthy. She'd put on extra pounds. And between Abby and her husband, their combined pay barely helped them get by. It certainly didn't cover the student loan payments and credit card debt they'd accumulated. It was a stressful place to be as a mom, as a wife and as an individual. To make matters worse, Abby was "living large" through the lives of her wealthy clients—even raising their children.

Then it struck her: she wanted that luxury lifestyle for herself, raising her own daughter with enough time and money to enjoy motherhood and entrepreneurship, too.

Wondering what more she could do, a chance meeting with another young woman while on a family vacation to Aruba provided the vehicle Abby was looking for: Isagenix. Though the two never spoke again, Abby followed the young woman on Facebook—watching with interest as she built a six-figure income and retired her husband from his corporate job.

"Do you remember me from Aruba?" Abby eventually messaged her, wanting to know how she and her family could have the same thing.

Starting on the Isagenix products made Abby feel like she was finally taking charge of her own future. *If these products work for me,* Abby thought, *I'll pursue this opportunity big time.*

But when Abby and her husband were visiting his aunt in Colorado—and Abby discovered Isagenix shake mixes in her kitchen—Abby quickly realized that Isagenix wasn't just for tired moms who needed to lose weight. The products were also being used by everyday people like her husband's aunt—a CrossFit fanatic—and by other athletes who loved its nutritional formula.

Once she saw Isagenix working for lots of other people, too, Abby was 1,000% committed to pursuing the business opportunity full-out. She also committed to playing a bigger game in her own life…and helping others play a bigger game in theirs.

"So many people are so beaten down by life or the economics of their situation," Abby says, "that they no longer have dreams. You can take a stand for people before they can ever take a stand for themselves. You can breathe life into them again."

Giving others permission to step into their own power—and do what's needed to make important changes in their life—is the most rewarding part of what Abby does. And it creates tremendous impact for the people she meets. In fact, just by allowing others to share what's going on in their lives, Abby often discovers a secret hardship that she—and the Isagenix lifestyle—can help with.

But the truly courageous part of what Abby does as an Isagenix leader is stepping up to rekindle a sense of excitement in people—that sense of destiny they had in their early years. It's a unique gift that Abby says top leaders should develop.

So what does she teach her own team about how to be this kind of transformational leader? *Cast a vision for people. Show them how to succeed.* Start building their belief in their own skills and capabilities by appreciating and acknowledging their positive qualities.

"Many people go through their lives unappreciated every day—like nothing they do is ever good enough," Abby says. One way to build a relationship and begin the transformation is to simply acknowledge the greatness within them, and ask questions like:

- What excites you?
- What would you be doing if you could do anything you wanted?
- What would that extra thousand dollars a month do for you?
- What would you and your family do if you had a month to go somewhere, such as staying in a beach house or spending a month in a villa in Tuscany?
- What would you feel like if you were doing those things?

Painting a picture, putting them in that place, not only helps them commit to playing a bigger game, it also helps them step up and match their work ethic to the size of their dreams.

Telling just one person a day, *You can do this,* Abby says, makes you a transformational leader. It's you putting your own cares aside to pour belief into someone else.

"The most transformational aspect of network marketing is that it allows anyone to become the grandest, most powerful and best version of themselves—even becoming someone they didn't know existed," Abby says. "This industry allows people to not only dream again, but also to learn about the work ethic and commitment that it takes to truly live out their vision."

"Love and compassion are necessities, not luxuries.
Without them humanity cannot survive."

—DALAI LAMA
Buddhist spiritual leader

LIFE IS A MOVING PARADE...KEEP ASKING

Our world is changing so quickly. Everyone needs to adapt. Take technology, for instance. When we started Isagenix, the iPhone was not invented. Today, every function imaginable is on our smartphones with new apps and social media platforms being developed every day. Automation, robotics, and AI—*artificial intelligence*—is changing the workforce and displacing millions of jobs.

No longer can we live with the status quo. We must wake up to this new reality, look into the future, and stay ahead of the curve. This means constantly pivoting and adjusting. Product innovation is key to ensuring our future, but so are technological enhancements. That's why Isagenix is continually evolving with new products and technology.

It takes courage and risk to reinvent. To create a legacy company, a team needs to solve problems, love challenges, and constantly make improvements. We have a huge responsibility and commitment to our Isagenix family—leaders who put their businesses and good name on the line every day. Their trust in Isagenix compels us to act with gratitude and a serving heart. Nothing will stop us from succeeding on their behalf. *Nothing.*

As I mentioned before, life is a moving parade. What works at Isagenix today will likely be upgraded, expanded or improved tomorrow. And just like companies change and grow, so do people's lives. What someone wasn't interested in six months ago might be ideal for them today. What they didn't need a year ago, they might be desperately seeking now.

Keep asking. Stay in touch. Always be interested in improving others' lives until the day when they are finally ready to make a change.

"If we did all the things we are capable of doing, we would literally astound ourselves."

—THOMAS A. EDISON

America's greatest inventor with more than 1,000 patents for devices such as the telegraph, motion picture camera, sound recorder and electric lights

---

HAVE THE COURAGE TO ASK PEOPLE TO JOIN YOU

In the first year of Isagenix, Jim and I travelled to Atlanta to do a meeting for a small group of emerging leaders.

At the end of the meeting, an energetic man came over and started to talk to me. He was so enthusiastic about our company and mission. He told me that evening that he was going to be the #1 income earner in Isagenix. He said, "Just watch me." He went to work and quickly rose to the top. Jimmy Smith has a heart of service and has helped everyone in Isagenix. He pours his love, passion, and belief into everyone. He is a true example of a servant leader.

At 92 years old, Jimmy has hundreds of thousands of people in his Isagenix organization. He was the company's first 20-star* Platinum, and he has created more Isagenix Millionaires than anyone else in the history of the company.** Together, Jimmy and his family are the #1 earners in the company and they've amassed more than $70 million in combined income over the past 18 years.

But life didn't start out that way. Jimmy's grandfather was a butcher, his father was a butcher, so naturally Jimmy thought he was destined to be a butcher, too. For 40 years, Jimmy worked as a butcher earning roughly

---

* *Awarded to associates who cycle 850 times or more per week.*

** *Results not typical.*

$10,000 per year during that time. Jimmy and his wife raised their six children on that butcher's salary.

To hear Jimmy tell it, for 40 years he lived "just over broke."

But all of that was about to change. Working in the shop one day, tragically Jimmy injured his back. *Disability,* the doctors eventually said. He was put out to pasture. All during the 1980's, Jimmy and his wife lived on meager finances until at age 62, he stumbled into network marketing.

"The idea that I could succeed if I helped other people succeed really appealed to me," Jimmy said.

For 12 long years—in company after company—Jimmy struggled, working hard to teach himself the industry until finally he was earning $5,000 a week. He knew his way around a compensation plan. He'd even gone bankrupt once with a company whose comp plan didn't pay off. But Jimmy was also street-smart, seasoned, and could assess the leadership of a company within minutes. In his mind, he was in a process of elimination, constantly researching new companies and always looking for a better bet.

"I had a friend who was doing well in the industry," Jimmy explains. "We always told each other that if we found the perfect company, we'd let each other know."

One day, the friend called about Isagenix. Her husband had done well on the products and Jimmy was willing to give it a try.

"I weighed 195 pounds at the time," he remembers. "Once I lost 21 pounds, I jumped in."

He drove over 1,000 miles to meet me and Jim in person.

"I fell in love with them," said Jimmy. "Their integrity, and their business acuity. Kathy and Jim weren't in it for the money. They were making a difference in the world. In the last 18 years, they have never missed a check, they have never been late, and the one time they were wrong was when they overpaid me."

Isagenix was the company he had been searching for, and in May of 2002 Jimmy Smith joined us in our dream to build the #1 company in the history of network marketing. People laughed when he told them he was walking away from $5,000 a week. They laughed again when he said he'd make $50,000 a week or more. It took a lot of courage to have those conversations. It took even more courage to ask friends and family to join him in yet another network marketing venture. But Jimmy knew Isagenix was the answer. And with the Isagenix compensation plan, he also knew he didn't need a lot of people to start off—just a few good people.

"The hardest thing we do is talk to people," Jimmy teaches his team. "The more people you talk to, the better you get at talking to people. The better you get at talking, the more people you will sign up."

Practice makes permanent, is the team's motto. Quitting is not an option.

Today, Jimmy Smith is one of the healthiest and most active 92-year-olds you'll ever meet. He wouldn't be the person he is today, he says, if it weren't for the Isagenix products.

Plus, he's a charmer.

"I've been in the company for 18 years," he begins, "and one thing about Kathy is that whenever you call her, she gets right back to you. She's so responsive. She's a people person."

Jimmy's told me countless times that his three biggest goals before he dies are to live to be 100 . . . have 100 grandchildren . . . and earn $100 million. With his lifetime of courage and a lifetime of helping people, I believe he will get there.

Being courageous isn't something we're born with. It comes from taking small risks and surviving them—even succeeding wildly as a result. While you should never risk imminent harm or financial ruin, here are three ways you can step up and be courageous.

Make a List of What's Not Working in Your Life

When was the last time you took inventory of your life? Are you satisfied with your finances, your career, your relationships, free time, health or lifestyle? One way to decide what's working your life—and what's not—is to take out a few sheets of paper (or your journal), and begin to think through each of the following areas:

- **Finances:** Are you satisfied with your income, debt load, expenses, monthly budget, and retirement savings? Have you set aside money for your kids' college expenses? Is your last will or trust completed? Do you have life insurance policies, long-term care insurance, or other life plans handled?

- **Relationships:** Are you happy in your marriage and in your relationship with your children? Do you feel supported and satisfied with the relationship you have with your parents, close friends, business partner, team, coworkers, employees, advisors or others you interact with regularly?

- **Health:** Are you in good health? Do you maintain an ideal weight? Have you resolved longstanding health conditions? Do you eat nutritious foods? Do you exercise regularly?

- **Career:** Are you satisfied with your job or business? Do you work with people who inspire and motivate you? Are you paid what you are worth?

- **Free Time:** Do you enjoy vacations, hobbies, "bucket list" adventures, date nights with your spouse, weekend travel, or other activities that contribute to a happy life and help you recharge for the workweek ahead?

- **Personal Growth:** Do you regularly learn new skills or expand your knowledge? Are you confident and fearless when taking on new tasks? Do you set goals and regularly achieve them?

When you've finished thinking through the categories above, write a plus sign ("+") next to those things that are stress-free, abundant, easy to manage, and fun for you. Put a minus sign ("–") next to those things that are stressful, difficult, need to be resolved, or simply aren't working. A plus-sign means, *Great! That's something that's working in my life,* while a minus-sign means, *Here's where I need to make a change.*

When we finally face what's not working, we often feel a sudden sense of relief. We can let go of that burden, stop losing sleep over it, and make plans to move forward toward a better life.

Set Goals for Making Important Changes

A lot has been written about how to set goals that are achievable. But a strategy I like was detailed back in 1981 in a *Management Review* article by George Doran. Not only should your most important goals be written down, but Doran said that goals should be:

Specific: State exactly what you will achieve, such as:
Pay off my mortgage.

Measurable: State how much you will complete, like:
... totaling $173,490.

Achievable: Make sure your goal can be achieved (even if you don't know how yet). Like this:
... by writing checks toward principal of $10,000 each.

Results-based: State how you'll know you've achieved it, such as:
... until I receive the cancelled note.

Time-limited: State the exact date by when you'll reach your goal. Like this:
... on or before June 30, 2024.

After following the steps above, your goal would look like this:

Pay off my mortgage totaling $173,490 by writing checks toward principal of $10,000 each, until I receive the cancelled note on or before June 30, 2024.

Choose One Action You Can Take...Then *Do It*

One of the easiest ways to make progress on your goals is to break them down into manageable daily tasks. If you decide that your most important health goal is to slim down and release toxins, you could enter the IsaBody Challenge and follow the guidelines for a specific period of time. If you decide that your most important financial goal is becoming debt-free, you could start with your car loan—creating a monthly budget that lets you spend only on your household needs, then applies leftover funds to making extra payments on the car.

Most self-help experts I've studied recommend using a sticky note, a daily journal entry, or a 3 x 5 card to write down your "must-do's" for the day—each a small step toward achieving your most important goals.

In the end, being courageous requires action. Until you take the first step, *nothing* in your life will change. And remember that, even when you do take action, achieving your goals usually takes time.

Persist until you succeed. Take action every day. Always have a can-do attitude. Success requires 100% commitment. Find a great mentor who will push you in good times and encourage you when times are tough.

Get your family involved in the process. Have regular family meetings—at least once a month. Share your goals for the business and how achieving those goals will affect your family. Plan rewards for yourself and rewards for your family, too, so that everyone is included and knows the payoff for reaching specific goals. I could have never been successful without the support of Jim and Erik—now we're working together to impact the world.

As we continue to grow and impact one country after another (with still more to come), we're continuously focused on our goals. Success takes time.

CHAPTER 5:

Have a Bold and Daring Goal

"Dream big. Start small.
But most of all, start."

—SIMON SINEK
Bestselling author of Start With Why
and Leaders Eat Last

As Isagenix grew and our results began to impact more and more people, I realized that it wasn't enough to have just daily goals or financial goals or company goals. I needed a *bigger vision* for my future work. I needed a goal that would create a powerful breakthrough and inspire others to play a bigger game, too—something different from anything I'd ever done.

In January 2014, we had a goal to take our company to $500 million in annual sales. We rallied the entire field of Isagenix associates around our vision, and called it The Paris Challenge.

$500 Million. Together We Will, was the slogan we used.

We promised that if Isagenix reached its goal of $500 million in sales (along with our associates' goal of increasing their own income), anyone achieving a certain benchmark would go with us on the trip of a lifetime to Paris, France—staying at the landmark Hotel George V just off the world-famous Avenue des Champs-Élysées.

Everyone pushed hard. In the end, together we did it! We reached the goal.

And just the memory of that trip…it was truly over the top. We showered our winners with lifetime experiences, treated them to a dinner cruise on the Seine River, and even included a $2,000 gift card from Louis Vuitton. But the highlight of the trip was a private dinner after closing hours at the Musée d'Orsay—home to the largest collection of impressionist art in the world. Without the crowds, our winners dined on fine French cuisine, then viewed priceless works of art by Monet, Degas, Van Gogh, and others. It was a fantastic once-in-a-lifetime experience.

Are these kinds of rewards part of the vision you have for *your* life?

When it comes to bold and daring goals, we should regularly ask ourselves, *What do I want to do next? What's the bold and daring goal that will shake things up, push me to learn new skills, and propel me to the next level? What excites me right now?*

"I GUARANTEE I'M GONNA WIN THE ISABODY CHALLENGE"

One bold and daring goal that's top-of-mind for many Isagenix associates is winning the IsaBody Challenge. Jim, Erik and I love the process of judging the finals. The contestants' stories are so compelling. One year, I'll never forget it, a man entered the room and lit everyone up with his passion, his results, and his excitement for the future. His energy was infectious, and—still to this day—he inspires thousands of people to go for their dreams and never let anything get in the way.

Growing up, Alvie Shepherd lived to play baseball. Whenever his older brother played a pick-up game with neighborhood friends, Alvie begged to be included. By the time he was 11, he was competing in velocity competitions for the fastest pitch. Eventually he became the fastest pitcher in the league. And when his dad finally took 12-year-old Alvie to a pro ball game at the local stadium in Chicago, Alvie vowed, then and there, that professional baseball would be his career.

All State. All Conference. A full-ride scholarship to University of Nebraska. Alvie won it all, until—out of the blue—he got an offer from the California Angels, his first chance at a career in Major League Baseball. Turning it down to go to college instead, Alvie racked up solid stats at the University of Nebraska until—by the time graduation arrived—he was widely seen as a first-round draft pick for a major league team.

Sitting at home with his brother on the day of the Major League Baseball Draft, Alvie waited breathlessly until finally the phone rang.

"Baltimore Orioles," said Alvie with emotion as he hung up the phone. "I just got drafted."

His agent negotiated a $750,000 contract. Alvie knew he had to perform. And just nine days before his call-up to the MLB, he pitched the best game of his life: eight innings, one hit, zero walks, and 10 strikeouts. The next day, however, Alvie got hit in the shoulder by an errant ball and, waking up the next morning, he could barely move his arm. Within days, instead of pursuing his dream as a pro ball player, he was off to rehab—working tirelessly to come back better than ever the next season. But it was no use.

Retired due to injury from his childhood dream at just 24 years of age, Alvie Shepherd's downward spiral began: too much alcohol, too much smoke-less tobacco, addicted to drugs and junk food—anything to mask the pain and disappointment. For 13 years, Alvie fought himself and, at one point, almost took his own life. Finally, at his lowest point and after a night of overdoing it with friends, Alvie suffered a brain aneurism and was rushed to the hospital by his girlfriend Rachel.

Coming out of emergency surgery and grateful to be alive, Alvie prayed fervently, *Thank you, Lord. I'm never going back.*

Released from the hospital on his 39th birthday, Alvie began to reclaim his health. He quit tobacco. He began to choose healthy foods. He went to the gym for the first time in 13 years. He wanted to marry Rachel and start a family. He wanted to be healthy in order to be a great role model for his kids.

After eight months of hard work and losing 40 pounds on his own, Alvie reconnected on social media with some former teammates and friends, one of whom was an Isagenix customer who—years after ending his athletic career—had a toned and ripped physique.

Alvie wanted that kind of healthy lifestyle and build for himself. And he also knew his ultimate goal: 204 pounds, his weight as a major league player.

"What exactly is Isagenix?" he asked friends on Facebook.

By the fifth day on the product, he felt amazing and already saw results on the scale. Within a month, he knew he had found his path back to being healthy and ripped. His mental state was solid. But the best part was, he had introduced some family members to Isagenix and made $750 his very first month as an associate—more than enough to pay for a month's worth of products with money left over. This, Alvie knew, was a new lifestyle he could latch onto and stick with. Plus, he entered the IsaBody Challenge to keep him accountable to reaching his goal.

Early in 2016, he posted a video to his Facebook page and declared his bold and daring goal to the world, "I'm gonna win the IsaBody Challenge."

On August 9, 2016, Alvie was voted the Grand Prize Winner. When he was announced as the winner in front of more than 10,000 fellow associates, he was more elated than the life-changing call he had gotten 21 years earlier: the Baltimore Orioles draft pick. He had come back from his deathbed. He had lifted himself from rock bottom. He had declared his bold and daring goal, and it had come true.

Alvie Shepherd gave credit to the Lord on stage as he accepted his $25,000 winner's check. He spent the next year traveling around the world to Isagenix events as an Ambassador for the IsaBody Challenge. Today, he teaches others to be open to being inspired again. He's personally enrolled over 130 former pro ball players—many of whom lost their identity and their health when they retired from the field, but regained it with Isagenix. But most importantly, today Alvie helps others live their best life and create bold and daring goals of their own.

"Goals help you channel your
energy into action."

—LES BROWN
Bestselling author, motivational speaker,
and talk-show host

STAY FOCUSED ON YOUR
DREAMS AND GOALS

For decades, scientists have studied not only how the brain functions, but also how it *helps us reach our goals.* One thing they know is that continually giving your brain a picture of what you want—by using a vision board, listening to a guided visualization, or concentrating daily on a 3 x 5 card where you've drawn or handwritten your goal—actually causes your brain to work day and night to bring about the exciting future you're focused on. In fact, when repeatedly filled with these vivid and colorful pictures of your spectacular future life, the brain actually becomes stressed over the difference between the way things are now and the way *you want them to be.*

Psychologist Leon Festinger first wrote about this phenomenon—called *cognitive dissonance*—in 1957. He compared it to the simple process of how your brain reacts when you're hungry: the brain sends signals to your body to eat—actually causing you to take those actions which will resolve your hunger. In the same way, when you begin focusing on your bold and daring goal—picturing this exciting new life in your mind—your brain will cause you to take those actions to resolve the discomfort and bring about this future.

What are some ways to focus on achieving your bold and daring goal? As I mentioned in the last chapter, start thinking about what you really want. Identify what's not working in your life and decide what you want to happen instead. This will give you a starting point—specific outcomes for you to focus on. What do you want your life to look like? What is your ideal dream?

Once you have your list of specific outcomes, commit to your bold and daring goal. Be willing to remove every obstacle to allowing it into your life. Then, keep a visual picture of your bold and daring goal in front of you—either by creating a colorful vision board or posting some other visual prompt where you'll see it often. I put my major goal on the bathroom mirror, refrigerator, inside my car windshield…everywhere!

"X" MARKS THE SPOT:
START CROSSING OFF YOUR GOALS

As I sat in the front row of a Super Saturday at our world headquarters, a beautiful lady came to the stage and shared her story. Seeing her passion, I thought, *Wow, what an outstanding goal and idea!* She got up and showed her vision board with all the debt she had acquired over the years. Her huge goal was to be debt-free. As Tammy Mould continued to make money, she paid off all her family's debts—marking off each with a big red X. What a great example for others to follow. *Believe it!* And you will achieve it.

One day at a time, Tammy Mould told herself. *Trust in God. Live the simple life.*

For four long years, Tammy's life had been a struggle between foreclosure, bankruptcy, bill collectors and a spiraling loss of hope that only desperation can bring.

But things hadn't always been that way.

For a few years, Tammy and her husband were living the good life—working hard to keep up with the Joneses. They'd moved into their dream home just outside Phoenix where Tammy had a home-based business in the network-marketing industry. Her husband James worked for a bank—a job he disliked, but it helped to pay the bills. Money was always in short supply. But with the small monthly pension Tammy's mother-in-law brought when she moved in with them, they were just able to get by.

Eventually, though, their fragile finances began to crumble. The network-marketing company that Tammy had built her business around announced they were changing their compensation plan—she would have to work twice as hard to make a lot less money. Additionally, Tammy's mother-in-law unexpectedly developed dementia and was moved to a nursing home for specialized care. And James was laid off from his banking job that summer.

"Things began to spiral," Tammy recalls. "We couldn't pay our bills. We couldn't afford the upkeep on the house. The stress was overwhelming. And here I was, trying to keep my small business earning enough to keep the lights on."

When Tammy walked outside one day to collect the mail, she turned and saw a Foreclosure Notice taped to their garage. Overcome with dread, she leaned against her car and vomited. Soon, creditors began to hound them and even called their neighbors. Week after week, Tammy and James sold off their belongings to pay the bills. But it was no use.

Bankruptcy was the only option left.

Downsizing into a $1,000 a month rental and trying to pick up the pieces of their lives, her husband got a new job as a teacher and after-school coach. He loved it. But the modest paycheck—combined with Tammy's dwindling earnings—still weren't enough to pay the bills of even their newly simplified life. Slowly, they began to live off their credit cards again, becoming The "No" Family—even saying no to attending church since they couldn't afford the gas to get there. What's worse, her family's health was starting to suffer under the strain. When her husband took on a third job—delivering newspapers in the early morning hours for extra cash—she could see him dying a little more each day.

Things had gotten as low as they could be. And for four long years, they stayed there.

Of course, the easy answer would have been to get a job. But Tammy had never been to college. Though she'd worked as an office clerk before the kids were born, she knew she didn't have the skills to go back into the workforce and command a good salary. Plus, it was the middle of a recession when millions were still unemployed. Network marketing was the only career where she had made any real money.

Even so, to make extra money during those lean years, Tammy worked once a week in her friend's catering business—getting paid on the spot, then driving her check to the bank to cash it in order to buy gas for her car. When her catering friend mentioned that she'd discovered Isagenix and was about to get involved, Tammy was interested but embarrassed. She didn't have the money to get started, even though she was convinced it was the path to better health for her family.

It's so unfair that all these people can get healthy, but not me, Tammy thought to herself. Shutting the door of her office, she broke down in tears. Enough was enough. That day, Tammy planned a brand new life for herself and her family. She wrote down dozens of goals including #32: *I want to get healthy for free.*

Confiding soon afterward to her mom about Isagenix, Tammy was humbled when her mother researched the company and their products—then sent a check to Tammy with a heartfelt letter, investing in their future because she'd seen the toll that financial hardship had taken on their health.

My prayer is that this endeavor will get you and James out of debt, she'd written. *I'm investing in your success because I love you.*

In less than two weeks on Isagenix products, Tammy could see the changes both in the mirror and in her outlook. She made $600 that first month which more than paid for future months' products. Slowly, she was meeting her goal: getting healthy for free. In the first year, Tammy lost 45 pounds and slimmed down to a healthy size 10.

Though they weren't out of debt yet, Tammy could see the light at the end of the tunnel. She dared herself to dream big. Taking out an oversized post-it note, she made a list of all their debts and bills—determined now to pay off every one. Whenever she made extra money through Isagenix, she would pay off a credit card and cross off the debt with a bright red Sharpie.

"No one knew about the list except me and God," Tammy explains. "Whenever I'd make extra money from the leadership pool, I would pay off a debt, then cross it off the list until there were red X's everywhere."

Within a year, she'd let go of her former network-marketing business, and in her second year with Isagenix—now earning *9x what she'd made the first year*—Tammy completely paid off the family's debts.

Her bold and daring goal had been achieved.

ALWAYS BE PUSHING TOWARD
YOUR NEXT GOAL

One of the biggest benefits of achieving your goals is that you instantly free up your focus to create and pursue new ones. I believe you should always be setting new goals for your brain to work on.

Why?

It turns out that the brain actually has a goal-seeking mechanism of its own: the *reticular activating system.* This system takes in all the information we're bombarded with every day—pictures, sounds, messages—then sorts through it all and identifies *what we need to know* in order to take action toward our goals.

If one of your goals, for example, is to add a hardworking new superstar to your organization, your brain might bring to your attention someone you met a few weeks ago through a friend or at a local event. And if your bold and daring goal is to retire your mom and buy her a house nearby, your brain would hone in on any conversation—even a casual one—about someone in your neighborhood who's about to make a move.

Additionally, since the brain is always at work creating new opportunities to achieve goals, we benefit greatly when we're always giving it new goals to work on. Goal-setting is not just a means to an end, it's an ongoing activity that will constantly improve your life. Plus, you're never too old to set an exciting new goal or dream an inspiring new dream.

"Things may come to those who wait, but only the things left by those who hustle."

—ABRAHAM LINCOLN
16th president of the United States

TAKE ACTION ON YOUR BOLD
AND DARING GOAL

When the opportunity does show up to achieve your goal, your job is to boldly step through that doorway and take action on the opportunity. In fact, taking action in the pursuit of their biggest goals is what makes top achievers different. They know that creating forward momentum is the most important thing they can do.

The same goes for your bold and daring goal, too.

When *you* make a start and begin to focus on your goal, a number of things will happen to support you in achieving it. First, you'll begin to "show up" differently: you'll glow with purpose and passion (which tells others that you're serious about your future). People will begin to notice the new energy and eventually see the new excitement in your appearance. You'll begin to *learn by doing* those skills that you cannot learn by merely researching or listening to others. Plus, you'll gain confidence with each new skill you're forced to acquire on the road to your goal. And you'll get advice about how to do things better, faster or more easily. Things that were difficult or scary before will become easier and almost second nature to you. But most importantly, you'll begin to attract people who will support and encourage you. Your momentum will become contagious.

No one can secure these benefits for you.

Only taking action on your bold and daring goal will help you become the kind of person who easily achieves even bigger and more inspiring goals. Only by taking action will you learn the habits and behaviors of goal-oriented people: rapid planning, taking small steps, adjusting to feedback, then moving forward with confidence.

"The big secret in life is that there is no big secret.
Whatever your goal, you can get there
if you're willing to work."

—OPRAH WINFREY
Billionaire talk-show host, actress, author and philanthropist

---

STAY FOCUSED ON YOUR GOAL

To help you stay focused on the daily tasks that lead to achieving big goals, there's a formula I teach to Isagenix associates: *Income Producing Activities.* As you go through your day, spend at least 80% of your time on activities that will bring you money: enrolling others, rank-advancing your team members, and training your team to stay focused themselves.

The key is to set realistic goals. Write them down and share them with your accountability partner. I recommend working in 30-day sprints.

Spend 80% of your time talking to new people, doing three-way calls with your team members, presenting the Isagenix product and business opportunity to others. How many times do you tell the Isagenix story? How many times is it being told by your team?

Plan your *Income Producing Activities* by adding numbers to the goal-setting checklist below:

- How many one-on-one presentations will I do?

- How many online product and business overviews will I do each week?

- Who are the people on my team who will run to the next rank with me, and who is running for the current company promotion?
  (Casting the vision that everyone will run together to win helps with the enthusiasm of the Team which is essential for your success.)

- How many new people will you enroll every month to reach your goal?

- How many new people will come into my team this month?
  (Everyone pushing to build the momentum makes it fun.)
- How many rank advancements will occur in my team this month?

What I love about network marketing is that you go up the ladder as you help people succeed.

MAKING AN IMPACT WAS HIS
BOLD AND DARING GOAL

This story is so inspiring. It just shows that if you have a bold goal and a burning desire to change your life, you can! With no special degrees in health or nutrition, Dave MacArthur raised himself up and now helps others go for their dreams. He has become an advocate for our anti-aging products, and teaches and trains our field on the power of proper nutrition.

His title 'Mechanic to Millionaire' is well-deserved. It shows that through focus, conviction, consistency and desire, anything is possible.

4:30 a.m. Time to get up. As a professional auto mechanic, Dave MacArthur worked 18 hours a day—delivering newspapers in the morning before fixing cars all day, then doing side jobs in the evening for extra money.

"There was never enough money to pay all the bills," Dave recalled. Like many families, Dave and his wife and five children were living paycheck to paycheck.

When he was younger, he daydreamed about the impact he would have on the world. While he loved working with his hands, he loved even more the idea of helping people, being of service, and changing lives for the better. In his heart, he knew that destiny was on its way. Someday—he didn't know when—an opportunity to do something heroic would appear.

Growing up, Dave's dad had instilled a strong work ethic in his 11 children. He was a schoolteacher, and talked often about the appreciation one receives when they work hard and serve others. Dave knew he wanted to receive that kind of appreciation himself. He lived the values of putting excellence into everything he did. He was honest, ethical, and naturally a hard worker.

But somehow, Dave's life had gotten off track. His David-and-Goliath ambitions kept getting pushed out further and further. He wasn't changing people's lives—he was changing the oil in their cars. Inside, he knew he had more to offer, but his circumstances made him feel trapped.

When did I lose sight of my dream? Dave wondered.

Equally deflating, Dave had also lost his health. He never felt well. He was always fatigued. Relying on coffee, energy drinks, stimulants and cold medicine to get through his day, Dave began to experience odd aches and pains. Robotically, he went through the motions every day.

Life should be abundant, shouldn't it? Dave thought. With his strong Christian faith, he believed that hard work and good values meant something. But he also knew he couldn't go on living this way. Not reaping the fruits of his labor was disheartening, frustrating…a downer.

Seeing him fade a little more each day, Dave's wife Cary signed them up for a self-help workshop where Dave learned how to dream again. He began to write down his ambitions and search for pictures he could look at regularly. Eight months later, they were attending a women's expo where Dave dropped his name in a fishbowl and won a free giveaway of Isagenix products.

"Do you feel that?!" Dave exclaimed to his wife on the third day of using the products.

For the first time in years, he felt good. He woke up with energy in the morning. His outlook was improving. He actually felt cheated for all the years he had suffered with fatigue. He eventually shed 53 pounds and got back to his high school weight. Plus, he even had the extra energy to take on more at work, return to being a model husband, and become an active citizen in his community.

When people began to approach him to ask what he was doing, Dave shared information about the Isagenix products to be helpful. Then others began referring their friends—they couldn't even pronounce the name! Dave didn't consider the Isagenix business opportunity all that interesting at the time, but he was thrilled that he got to coach people.

Finally he was helping to change lives.

Soon, he wanted to do more. Attending an Isagenix meeting, he learned about the science behind the products and realized that Isagenix could literally transform lives. He wanted to teach people and help them make lifelong behavioral changes. He put together a PowerPoint presentation about what he'd learned and began to do meetings in people's homes.

In just five short months, Dave fully replaced the combined income he was making from the auto shop, his newspaper route, and his side jobs. Before long, he and his family moved into their dream home. And in 15 years with Isagenix, he's earned nearly $10 million in personal income—sometimes making as much in 10 days as he used to make in a whole year.*

Coming from a place of limited means—living paycheck to paycheck, year after year—Dave's bold and daring goal back then was simply to have enough money to afford the little luxuries of life: taking his wife to dinner and a movie, buying his kids new clothes instead of waiting for hand-me-downs, getting new tires for the family car instead of buying retreads. *Let me just be a good provider to start with,* was Dave's bold and daring goal.

But gradually, as his Isagenix income grew, Dave's natural affinity for serving people re-emerged. His next bold and daring goal was to become a leading Isagenix speaker and educator—a dream that came true when he was asked to be the opening keynote speaker in front of 14,000 people at Isagenix's annual Celebration event. As he prepared to go on stage, Dave thought briefly of an evening during his childhood when—passing through the family room—he saw the legendary motivational speaker Zig Ziglar on television. *You'll do this one day,* said a voice inside him. From that day forward, Dave has always

---

* *Results not typical.*

believed his destiny was to be a teacher and educator—serving people and helping them make behavioral changes.

Today, with thousands and thousands of people on his Isagenix team, that destiny has become a reality.

And his next bold and daring goal?

Growing people—hand-in-hand with God—as he improves their lives physically, mentally and financially. In his mind's eye he can see the ripple effect at work: people on his team creating 10 times the impact that Dave originally did. Dave MacArthur *knows* that people have greatness within them. He wants to unleash that greatness by giving people the confidence and daring to go for their own dreams—as he once did.

> *"The two most important days in your life*
> *are the day you are born and the*
> *day you find out why."*
>
> —MARK TWAIN
> *American writer, humorist, entrepreneur and lecturer*

CELEBRATE SMALL WINS AND REWARD YOURSELF FOR THE BIG ONES

When we do achieve a goal, however small, it's important to celebrate. Why? Because it trains our subconscious mind that, at the end of all that hard work, there's a reward, a payoff, or something fun. Just like a mom who promises her toddler that they'll go to the park if he'll behave while she's working, the "inner child" in our brain will do the same thing if there's something fun at the end of the behaving.

Make sure to take the time to celebrate *every* win—even if it's just getting a massage or facial, or some fun retail therapy like buying a new pair of shoes. Perhaps it's a special date night with your spouse to thank them for their support...or celebrating with your family by vacationing at a favorite amusement park.

I also got Erik and Jim into celebration mode with me, and it made them feel part of the fun.

Our amazing company does many special things for our associates when they reach a new rank: trips like visiting Head Office to be trained by our most successful people or special events in our home to recognize their achievement. We also host many promotions for our members so they can go on dream vacations to destinations like the Cayman Islands, Hawaii, Rome, and even Fiji.

Erik once created a special event for Millennials to travel to Peru and visit Machu Picchu. Additionally, they helped native people with their children and got to experience what it's like to live in a local community.

These are trips of a lifetime that most people would never experience.

It's also important to get your family members involved in your celebration plans. Why? They can help you (and push you) to take the steps needed to meet your bold and daring goal. When you *do* reach your goal, reward yourself, but be sure to reward your family, too.

What are some other ways to make your bold and daring goal a turning point in your successful life?

Create a Bold and Daring Goal That Inspires You

Think about what you want to achieve. *Would I be happy if. . .?* we should ask ourselves.

Is it becoming debt-free or achieving ideal health or buying your dream home? Many Isagenix associates say that giving their parents the good life in their golden years is a major motivator. Whatever inspires you, write it down, create a vision board of images and words, or put it on a 3 x 5 card or a sticky note that you can look at frequently.

Identify What You Need to Do to Achieve That Goal

The achievement of every goal starts with your mindset: if you believe it, you can achieve it. The key is to identify those actions that are required to achieve your goals—then write them down. This written list of actions not only gives you a daily to-do list to accomplish, it also forces you to investigate the process and better understand how to get from your starting point to the end goal. That understanding is knowledge you can take to the next goal...and the next.

Of course, an important part of the goal-centered mindset is the *purpose* behind the goal. For your largest goals—goals that can elevate others—ask yourself, *What value will achieving this goal bring to other people?* There is magic in thinking big and considering the benefits beyond just yourself and your family.

When you do think big, be sure to leverage all the resources you can think of including other business leaders who might want to be involved. You'd be surprised how inspiring your goals might be to people outside your circle—if enough people would be positively impacted or if it lets other people achieve their own similar goal. While they might have been thinking the same way, they may not have fully researched the goal or assembled the necessary resources. The fact that *you have done* this advance work makes working with you more appealing.

Be sure to share your goals with your family, too. After all, the outcome will likely benefit them—and they may be able to help you with more ideas, but also support you in staying focused.

And, believe me, your most important goals deserve your focus in the same way that they deserve bold, massive action.

Use Your Time Wisely

Of course, allocating time to focus on our goals is essential. One of my favorite books is *The 10X Rule: The Only Difference Between Success and Failure* by Grant Cardone. And one of my favorite take-aways from the book is that we should all ask the question: *Is what I'm doing right now the best use of my time?* Will the activity you're in the middle of right now get you *closer* to your goal—or *keep you* from getting there? If we all asked this question a lot more as we go through our day, we wouldn't spend time on unproductive activity.

There are also other mistakes we wouldn't make, like these that are on my personal checklist:

- Setting objectives that are too low

- Underestimating the actions and resources necessary

- Underestimating the challenges you will need to overcome

When you maintain a "can do" attitude and believe that you can figure out the solution to any roadblock, your confidence will soar. When you focus on your opportunities, learn to love challenges, and persist until you are successful, achieving goals will become easier over time.

Any goal requires your full commitment to succeed.

Use Affirmations to Keep You Focused

Whenever I'm working toward a goal, I'm obsessed with achieving the outcome I've visualized. Having a clear picture in your mind of the ideal outcome is key. For years, I've used powerful visual triggers called *affirmations* when going for any new goal.

Affirmations are richly descriptive statements of the emotions you would feel and the things you would be doing if your goal had already been achieved.

I am attracting the most amazing new leader to my team, and I feel their excitement, is one example of an affirmation. *I'm happily writing a check for the final payment on my student loan,* is another.

Remember the brain's *reticular activating system* I talked about earlier? Affirmations help the brain focus on a crystal-clear image of what you want. Write down your goals in a journal, on 3 x 5 cards, or on your vision board using vivid descriptive language. Read them several times a day. Feel the emotions you would be experiencing if that goal had already come to pass. Then, let your brain help you determine the path you'll take to get there using all the resources at your fingertips.

Track Your Progress Using Key Performance Indicators

As you take massive action, be sure to keep track of your success. If your goal is to eliminate a major debt, count down the balance remaining as you make payments. If your goal is to build an investment portfolio, look at your numbers frequently. The oft-quoted Karl Pearson, English mathematician and founder of the discipline of *mathematical statistics,* said, "That which is measured improves." It's true. In fact, in business, companies typically measure their *key performance indicators* to help them determine whether they're on track to meet their goals. You, too, can use KPI's to measure your progress.

If you know, for instance, that you need to talk to 100 people in order to enroll 12 new associates, then *Number of People I've Presented to This Week* might be a key performance indicator for you. Monitor your numbers and you'll stay focused on making progress. If you fall short one week, make adjustments to your approach, your schedule or your focus.

Work With an Accountability Partner to Keep You on Track

One of the best-kept secrets of super successful Isagenix associates is *working with an accountability partner.* When you team up with someone who also has big goals, you can keep each other accountable for meeting deadlines, doing what's necessary, and reaching milestones.

Be sure to choose someone who will hold your feet to the fire and keep driving you forward. Schedule regular calls (at least weekly) that are 15 minutes or less, and that are designed *only* to report on what you have accomplished since the last call—no chatting about family life or giving advice. The goal here is to talk regularly with someone who knows your dreams and ambitions—and who won't let you get away with falling down on the job. When you know you have to check in with someone on a certain day to report on your progress, you're much more likely to finish your to-do list, make those calls, and spend the time necessary to meet your goals.

Our Isa Rally promotions have proved successful in helping to support team development and accountability.

In the end, the only person responsible for achieving your goal is *you*. You must assume 100% responsibility for your success. Never blame other people when your goal fails to materialize. Look at yourself in the mirror and ask yourself what part you played in the outcome. Then be open to adjusting your actions to produce a better outcome.

CHAPTER 6:

Do "The Do"

"Focus on doing the right things, instead of a bunch of things."

—MIKE KRIEGER
Co-founder of Instagram

As the waiting line for the Leadership Training at Isagenix's global Celebration conference wound its way through the main foyer of the Music City convention center in Nashville, an expectant buzz went through the associates who had qualified to be let in.

They were about to learn privileged information from the company's top earners on how to build their businesses, train their teams—even how to leverage current trends and technology. Our corporate staff had selected speakers who were growing and totally engaged in their business.

Now, as the leaders eagerly filed in, a DJ playing hip-hop music greeted them, along with five Jumbotron screens designed to serve an audience that was packed as far as the eye could see.

Slowly, the lights dimmed and our first panel of leaders took the stage to reveal their strategies. It was time to do "The Do."

WHAT DOES IT MEAN TO DO "THE DO"?

The fundamentals of building a network-marketing business are simple. In fact, when you are helping to change people's lives, it's so exhilarating that it doesn't feel like work at all.

But while the fundamentals are simple, it still takes time to develop the skills necessary to succeed. Just like any career or sport or activity, to get good at it you have to practice, practice, practice.

Execution is everything. That's what it means to *do The Do*.

While most people are used to reporting to a boss, now *you* are the boss—and responsible for your own success. That success (or lack of it) will depend on how consistently you do the *Income Producing Activities* that I talked about earlier.

Enrolling new members, then casting the vision of possibilities to your new team members is crucial. The key is to help your people rank advance—that is, go Manager, Director, and Executive. Then the magic happens: you rank advance to a high rank.

It's not about mass marketing. It's about getting your team to duplicate.

If you're working hard to win an incentive trip to Fiji, your team is going to follow your lead. They will do what you do. If you stay focused on getting to the next rank, they will focus, too.

That's duplication.

Network marketing is simply building a network of people who buy and consume the best products in the world. You refer people to your online business to purchase products, and they refer people *they know* to do the same. This network is your asset.

Training should be the next component of your activities. Train your new members on the products and the compensation plan, then teach them how to present the products and business opportunity to others.

It takes a lot of energy to launch a network-marketing business. Think about how an airplane takes off from the runway: massive acceleration is needed. The same is true for launching your business. Speed is everything!

The faster you can duplicate these necessary steps, the more people you will introduce to Isagenix, and the easier it will become:

- Find new people who might have an interest
- Talk to people about Isagenix
- Present the Isagenix opportunity
- Follow-up with any additional information they need
- Enroll them
- Help them get started successfully as an Isagenix Associate
- Promote events so you can present the Isagenix opportunity to more people at the same time
- Always be sure to ask for referrals. For example: *"I know you know a lot of people. Maybe you can help me. I just started my business,*

*and I'm looking for people who want to change their position in life.
Do you know anybody who's looking for better health or additional
income?"*

What I love about this profession is that you succeed when you help others become successful! Unlike the corporate world, where you succeed at the expense of someone else, network marketing is about helping others learn, improve and apply what they know. People rarely take action if they lack confidence—they gain confidence by doing The Do.

Think of Isagenix as a personal-growth journey with a compensation plan attached. You'll learn so many life skills you can use throughout your day—invaluable lessons that will stay with you for good!

---

*"Doing the best at this moment puts you in the
best place for the next moment."*

—OPRAH WINFREY
Billionaire talk-show host, actress, author and philanthropist

---

ONE MORE REASON TO DO "THE DO":
800 MILLION PEOPLE ARE ABOUT TO EMBRACE
A NEW WAY OF EARNING A LIVING

In 2017, McKinsey & Company—the global consulting firm whose research division produces influential reports on trends and management topics—published a study that rocked the world's major economies. By 2030, it said, *400 million to 800 million workers will be displaced* by automation, artificial intelligence and robotics. But this time, the wage earners losing their jobs won't all be factory workers with repetitive skills—but college-educated, white collar professionals whose high salaries and expensive benefits make employers eager to replace them with robots, algorithms and cloud computing. Architects, payroll managers, engineers, IT professionals—even artists, designers and media executives—these are the types of high-paying jobs that the McKinsey study says will experience a decline as countries rapidly automate.*

The good news for Isagenix associates willing to do The Do is that the vast majority of these workers will be looking for a new way to earn a living.

Doing what?

If we look at the limited ways these educated professionals have to replace their six-figure incomes, only one path becomes clear: *network marketing.* It doesn't require expensive schooling to retrain for a different profession. It doesn't require years of starting over in an entry-level position at the few companies willing to hire them. And it doesn't offend their sense of self-worth and independence since network marketing combines the real possibility of earning what they're worth with being respected by their peers, friends and customers.

"We estimate that between 400 million and 800 million individuals could be displaced by automation and need to find new jobs by 2030 around the world."

—McKINSEY & COMPANY
Global management consulting firm

BECOME A LEADER WORTH FOLLOWING

I remember our very first Executive Training in January of 2004. I was in front of the room training our most successful associates when a woman stood up and said, "I'm going to do this. I am ignorance on fire, but nothing is going to stop me."

---

* *Read the McKinsey & Company study at* https://www.mckinsey.com/featured-insights/future-of-work/jobs-lost-jobs-gained-what-the-future-of-work-will-mean-for-jobs-skills-and-wages

That was the beginning of Susan Sly's journey to success in Isagenix. She rapidly moved up the ladder and now has one of the most successful teams in the company. She has that all-important "can do" attitude, and has inspired so many women to go for their dreams. She is more committed than ever to creating six- and seven-figure earners. What I respect most about Susan is her dedication to *servant leadership*. She helps everyone in Isagenix and treats their success like it's her own company.

By anyone's definition, at just 27 years old, Susan Sly had it all. She was slim, attractive, and successful—a media personality in her home country of Canada. Like many women, she also did it all: awake by 4:00 a.m. to open the health club she owned and manage her staff before teaching nutrition at the local college by mid-day. She was a certified holistic nutritionist...a professional triathlete...did three workouts a day...had her own personal-training clients...recorded three to four pieces for television some days...and had a regular radio show on Sunday mornings. She was also a mom and a wife—and she was exhausted.

From the outside, Susan had all the trappings of an extraordinary life. But inside, she was suffering. She began dropping things, got headaches, and regularly felt tingling in her hands and feet. After a battery of medical tests, her doctor called her in for the results: Susan had MS—*multiple sclerosis*—one of the worst cases he'd ever seen.

To add to her stress, her marriage was falling apart.

She was broken, overwhelmed and weary, and in that moment, she got down on her knees and begged, *Lord, if you show me the way, I'll do the work.*

Three months later, she met a new personal-training client—a woman who introduced Susan to the idea of network marketing. She constantly talked about it, but Susan—as a professional athlete, nutrition expert, and media personality—thought network marketing had no place in her career. Plus, she had slowed her schedule considerably, didn't want to add more work, and still traveled extensively. In fact, she was scheduled to go to Malaysia for an Ironman competition. But in the course of training harder than ever, she fractured her pelvis on a training ride.

"Why are you working at the club today?" the woman asked Susan with concern. "It's because you don't have residual income."

It was a wake-up call for Susan, who had built her multiple businesses on exchanging time for money.

Handing Susan a copy of Robert Kiyosaki's book, *Rich Dad Poor Dad,* the woman gently urged Susan to work on herself, her outlook and her attitude. While Susan eventually joined the network-marketing company the woman recommended, it really wasn't the right fit. Susan was used to playing a bigger game, and the lack of potential she experienced with the company made her feel . . . small.

In fact, by the time Susan was three years into her diagnosis, she realized that—for the first time in her life—she had settled for less than her dreams. She had resigned her life to dying from MS, and—though she was remarried, with a daughter and new baby—she was suffering in silence. The only happy thought she had in those days was to take her own life. She was cynical, skeptical, disappointed—and out of solutions. She actually believed her kids would be better off without her.

On the day she planned to end her life, her daughter stayed home sick from summer camp. With her opportunity interrupted, Susan forced herself to keep going—and that was the day she decided to take a look at Isagenix. Reading the product's ingredient list, she was impressed. It was a beautiful depth of nutriceuticals put together by master formulator John Anderson.

Then she remembered: at the peak of her athletic career in the early 90's, she was fueling her body with one of John's early formulations. Within days of starting on the Isagenix products, she felt dramatically better. In fact, she woke up on Day Four and—looking in the mirror—felt joy.

For the first time in years, she liked who she saw.

She had nearly lost everything. Now Isagenix had brought her back into the light. But she also realized that, through her work as a fitness expert and nutritionist, she had met thousands of women who, like her, were struggling and overwhelmed—not just with their fitness and their weight, but with life in general.

"We don't need to feel this bad," she began to tell them. With Isagenix, she knew she had a product that would change their life *and* their legacy. She could feel her passion and purpose returning.

Let me find just ten women, she declared as her very first goal, *and turn them into six-figure earners.*

Today, Susan Sly has helped 44 people achieve the title of Isagenix Millionaire—with almost half of them joining her team during the 2008 Recession. Though she had nearly lost everything, with Isagenix, she made a turnaround.

"As you grow older, you will discover that
you have two hands, one for helping yourself,
the other for helping others."

—AUDREY HEPBURN
British actress, fashion icon and humanitarian

THE PEOPLE YOU'RE LOOKING FOR
ARE ALSO LOOKING FOR YOU

When Susan stepped onto the stage in Nashville to train Isagenix's top leaders, she shared real-world strategies for building an organization and attracting others you *want* to work with. Here's her advice:

People aren't buying shakes, and they're not buying you. When someone considers becoming an Isagenix customer or associate, what are they actually buying? Certainty.

Certainty comes from how confident that person is in *your belief.* What is your belief in your ability to successfully launch someone into Isagenix?

Additionally, Susan explained, "Underlying certainty is hope. When you lead with certainty, you also help transform hope into confidence."

Mind the gap. Not every Isagenix associate has the ability to lead a conversation around money, but anyone can identify "gaps" in the prospect's lifestyle, finances or goals that aren't being met now—but which could be met through the Isagenix business opportunity.

Be nimble and identify these gaps, Susan says, then lead the conversation by presenting Isagenix as a solution to their current problem or goal. Serve them out of love and empathy for their situation.

Attach meaning to the money. When talking to a potential new associate for your team, zero in on one financial burden they'd like to handle, Susan suggests.

Do you have a bill that keeps you up at night? you might ask. *What if Isagenix could help you pay that one bill?*

Between June and November, a new associate on Susan's team paid off her entire student loan. Now, when Susan teaches the compensation plan, she attaches meaning to the money and hones in on what those monthly Isagenix earnings might mean to the prospect.

The people you're looking for are looking for you. If you want to attract business builders, be an aggressive business builder yourself. Ambitious entrepreneurs are attracted to someone who's building and succeeding.

If you want someone who is coachable and who'll do what's necessary to succeed, be coachable and driven yourself.

Susan has an acronym she uses when looking for the ideal Isagenix associate: "CCDT" which stands for *comfortable, capable, desire* and *time*. Are they *comfortable* when leading and prospecting? Are they *capable* of executing what you're asking them to do? Do they have the *desire* to reach big goals? Are they willing to carve out the *time* necessary?

"Helping people who have those four attributes is where I spend 80% of my time," says Susan.

The most important person we have to recruit every day is ourselves. Perhaps the most important success principle that Susan shared with us on stage that day is the importance of *working on yourself.* Be focused with your time, clear about your goals, and ready to do what's necessary.

The average person wakes up and looks at other people's lives online before they ever look in the mirror—before they even plan to make progress in their own life that day. Susan recommends instead that you take the first 45 minutes every morning to ground yourself and get into the right "head space" for success. Read, meditate, spend time in prayer, listen to an inspiring podcast, do some journaling—anything that will focus you on what you need to accomplish that day. Be sure to spend a few minutes every morning managing your time, too. If there's something on Susan's schedule that doesn't serve her purpose that day, for example, she'll reschedule it in order to stay focused.

When the day is done, ask yourself, *Who did I serve today? How did I add value today? What do I need to accomplish tomorrow?*

"There are so many people who are relying on your leadership qualities," Susan admonishes. ""Where will you be if you can't even lead yourself?"

> *"Surround yourself with only people who are going to lift you higher."*
>
> —OPRAH WINFREY
> *Billionaire talk-show host, actress, author and philanthropist*

SURROUND YOURSELF WITH POSITIVE PEOPLE

I once heard a quote that has stayed with me since the early days of my career: *You are the average of the five people you spend the most time with.*

It's true.

So who are *you* allowing to influence you, advise you, and cheerlead for you—someone who is positive and wants the best for you... or someone who is constantly criticizing, nay-saying, or making you feel guilty about your goals?

It's time to surround yourself with positive people and limit your exposure to toxic, negative people who can always find something to complain about (including every reason under the sun why *your* ideas, goals and dreams won't work or aren't important).

Find possibility thinkers who are focused on success. People who talk about what's possible, who have ambitious goals of their own, and who pro-actively discuss how to overcome obstacles are classic *possibility thinkers*. They're focused on good outcomes for everyone. They're capable, smart and resourceful. And they're a lot of fun to be around.

So where can you find them?

There are lots of *possibility thinkers* in Isagenix—usually in leadership roles with teams who love to learn from them. In fact, one thing we emphasize in Isagenix is personal-growth training, including developing a can-do attitude, finding your own motivation, and having a preference for taking action.

Outside of Isagenix, you can read books by human-potential experts, attend self-help trainings, or find positive groups of people on social media.

Avoid toxic people. Just like the speedboat I mentioned earlier—surging through the water, creating a wake of activity, achievement and impact in its path—our lives also have *motors, controls* and *anchors*.

While motors keep us driving forward and controls help us maintain our focus, *anchors* simply hold us back and keep us stationary. We have no use for an anchor when our speedboat is surging forward.

Well, some of the people in our lives are like those anchors. They're holding us back and keeping us from growing—through their negativity, criticism, and manipulation. They remind us of all the times we failed. They give us their "seasoned advice" on topics they know nothing about. And they try to reset our priorities to ones that they approve of.

Stop doing what you're doing, they seem to say, *and come do what I want you to do.*

Of course, toxic people aren't always deliberately spiteful and negative —sometimes they simply have a subconscious fear that we're growing and pulling away from them. They take up our time and our focus, almost as a defense mechanism—but the result is the same: their demands rob us of our future. These are the "time bandits" that productivity experts warn us about. Instead of giving into their invitations for "lunch with the gang" or letting them drag you into another conversation about the latest fight with their spouse, just say no. If you feel that an explanation is needed for your refusal (it's not), simply tell the truth: it's important for you and your family's future to stay focused on your goals. As Jack Canfield, in *The Success Principles,* likes to say: *I'm over-committed as it is. It's not against you, it's for me.*

If you can't find positive people in your own circle of friends and family members, "borrow" them from someone else. Before you've built your own network of positive people, you can find successful people to follow, listen to, and admire. And you may even meet someone who can mentor you as you grow.

Many of the top Isagenix leaders hold regular trainings to keep you inspired, informed and focused on achieving the life of your dreams. Exposure to personal-growth training is essential to your success and can help you make new contacts and build relationships which are crucial. That's exactly what happened to me when I went to an event in Dallas and met David Wood who, at the time, was the lead trainer for T. Harv Eker. After the event, we met for lunch where we masterminded many ideas. Due to that meeting, David became a part of Isagenix and has impacted the movement and culture we've created at the company. He's created several training programs including *Journey to the Stage* and *University in Action.* He travels all over the world instilling our culture in our members. And he's a master at helping people develop the skills necessary to be successful. Not only that, but he's also become a mentor to our Executive Team, as well as many members—making a huge impact on so many of our leaders.

In the same way we have added David to our team, remember to surround *yourself* with a good team, too. Find people who have the skills that you don't have, so you all complement each other. Collaboration is the key to success!

Finally, choose your advisors wisely. One of the unique characteristics of successful people is that they're very choosy about the experts they listen to for advice—whether it's related to business growth, tax planning, finance and investing, maintaining a great marriage, or something else that's personal and unique to their situation. To step up and begin acting like a top leader well before you reach significant monthly earnings, why not begin researching and seeking out smart, successful leaders who can guide you and educate you in building an extraordinary team? When you do get good advice from them, follow it. And make sure to get a great financial advisor to help you plan for your successful business.

"There is a difference between giving directions and giving direction."

—SIMON SINEK
Bestselling author of Start With Why *and* Leaders Eat Last

WHO SHOULD BE THE <u>MOST</u> POSITIVE PEOPLE IN YOUR LIFE?

Your family. When everyone is working toward a common goal, but also feels that their own dreams are important, a family can soar together. When chaos and drama are gone, and family members are happy and growing, a positive outlook is almost certain. Whether you have a spouse and kids—or whether you're single and your "family" is your siblings, parents and closest friends—you need their support to create the future you envision for yourself.

So how can you inject optimism and possibility-thinking into your family life?

Start with a family meeting where together you create shared goals you can all support. Perhaps building your Isagenix business is the key to eliminating crushing debt or sending your kids to private school. Let everyone know what they can do to support achieving that goal.

Something else you can do is to teach your children to stay positive in the face of their own journey of learning and doing new things as they grow up. Transform "failures" into learning opportunities and teachable moments. Teach planning skills, goal-setting, creative problem-solving, and—most important—that there's more than one way to achieve a goal.

Text your teenager an "inspiration for the day"—either a quote or saying you've heard—to help them think about their future, stay strong under peer pressure, or simply lighten their day.

Finally, *stay positive yourself.* Imagine how much positive thinking would rub off on your spouse and kids if nothing is ever a problem, the future is always sunny, and every situation has a silver lining—simply by creatively looking at ways to turn lemons into lemonade.

In addition to helping your family stay positive, there are other family lessons I've learned over the years:

Put your family first. It's easy to get caught up in your Isagenix business and assume that your family life is balanced, supportive...solid. But that isn't always the case. Aging parents, teenagers, young children—they all need our attention, as well as our flexibility to drop-and-handle whatever comes up. Luckily, the network marketing model gives you the kind of time freedom you need to put your family first, then tend to your business and team once the crisis is over.

Even without a problem to solve, be sure to schedule family time on your calendar. If it's not booked, a thousand other things can take up your time and crowd out the special family moments that lead to a close, loving, supportive family life.

Take care of your spouse. Respect and gratitude must come first in a marriage. And creating the ultimate relationship takes time.

Communication is one of the most important things. Find out what their dreams are. What gets them excited about the future? What would our ideal life look like together?

As a couple, have goals that you establish together, then celebrate wins.

Always be a good listener, and I mean *really* listen. Ask questions that dig deeper so you know what they want and what makes them happy. In fact, both of you should not only get good at listening—but more importantly, you should get good at sharing your concerns in a constructive way. Be a problem-solver. If you're having a challenge, say, "I really need your help. Can we set aside some time together to talk?"

Consider how this challenge will affect the relationship. Grow together in your ability to solve problems.

"Let's work through this together," you can assure your spouse. That's showing respect for your spouse and trusting them with suggesting an outcome that's acceptable to you both.

It's what the closest of friends would do, and your spouse should be your best friend always.

You can also take a class together, growing or improving in some way. Jim and I took a massage class together, and it was amazing. It brought us closer, and continually helps create the intimacy necessary for a relationship.

Plus, here's my additional advice on husbands: Always express gratitude to your husband in private *and* in public. Compliment him when he does great things for the family. Tell him how much you appreciate him. When I take Jim his coffee in the morning, I tell him, "You are the best husband. We're going to have an amazing day."

This one comment changes everything and sets the day up right. Try it—it works! Find something to compliment regularly. Look for the good. You can even compliment him in public—*Thank you for being the best ever,* you might say. *I love you so much*—making him feel cherished and appreciated.

Of course, it goes without saying that, as a couple, you should make sure to have special time together when it's just you and your spouse. Take time for romance, creating special times that you will never forget. Make special dinners, and celebrate every year you are together.

Make your children your best friends. While you should always put your spouse first, don't wait for an opportunity to focus on building a "best friend" relationship with your kids, too.

One of the most rewarding things I've ever done was to be a mom and teach Erik important values: a can-do mindset, how to set goals, how to think of others, how to handle finances, and how to make ethical decisions. At some point, your children will become adults, and the foundational work you've done—along with being a good role model yourself—will help transform their childhood relationship with you into one where they share with you, confide in you, and include you in their plans.

In contributing to this book, Erik shared, "My mom is an extraordinary human being and the most generous person I've ever known. She is generous with her time, attitude, resources, and her willingness to serve when she doesn't have to. She's an incredible mom. And I'm so incredibly grateful that I get to work alongside my parents and learn from them every day. Everything that's good in my life is coming from what they created with Isagenix."

Thank you, Erik. Being your mom is the biggest joy in my life.

"Leadership is not about glorious crowning acts.
It's about keeping your team focused on a goal and
motivated to do their best to achieve it...
It is about laying the groundwork for others' success,
and then standing back and letting them shine."

—CHRIS HADFIELD
Commander of the International Space Station

SYSTEMATICALLY BUILD
A SUSTAINABLE NETWORK

For years, I'd known about Susan Miller's astounding success in the network marketing field. When I called her in the early days of Isagenix, however, she wasn't open. Eventually, we spoke again and she finally took a look due to her trust in Jim and me and a former business relationship of Herb and Patty Cepeda.

Susan came to world headquarters and loved what we were doing to make network marketing a respected profession, and she especially fell in love with our compensation plan.

"Finally," she said, "someone got it right."

She already had everything it takes to become successful. She was smart, successful, driven—and so committed to making Isagenix her final network-marketing home and create a legacy for her family.

When I first called Susan to ask her to take a look at Isagenix, I knew she was the amazing leader that everyone said she was. Smart, focused, entre-preneurial—what every network-marketing company wants at the head of one of their most successful teams.

But Susan was not open at first.

Years of successfully building and rebuilding large organizations—only to see them fall apart—had destroyed her belief in the network marketing model. It was simply too hard for the masses to duplicate. There had been too many tripwires where Susan's team didn't get paid. As it turns out, Susan learned, practices like these were common in the industry.

At just 34 years old, she was done. She didn't want to fight the uphill battle any longer.

Of course, things hadn't always been that way. Starting out as a hairdresser in south Florida, Susan quickly learned that trading time for money behind the chair at a salon wasn't going to get her very far, so she launched her own successful personal care company in the salon industry. Her husband Murray was a business owner, too. When a friend introduced her to a business opportunity for a hair-regrowth product, Susan realized it was a direct-selling company. She wasn't interested. She had her own business to run. But for the sake of the friendship, she attended an opportunity meeting anyway.

Seeing 350 people in the room, Susan took notice. She leaned in. The people talking on stage were from all walks of life: a real estate agent, a finance guy. *What?* They talked about trends and timing and getting onboard at the front of the train.

Susan was in awe. She immediately understood the business model. She realized that anyone willing to do the work could develop a network, build a virtual company without all the hassle of overhead and responsibility, and earn residual income, too. In her experience, that simply wasn't available to everyday people. She knew she could be a success.

For the next eight months, she threw herself into the business. The network marketing industry was her focus and joy. All she had to do was block out the noise and *do the do*. By the end of eight months, she had replaced her full-time income spending just six to ten hours a week sharing the product and opportunity. Three months later, she doubled her income. On word of mouth alone, the growth potential was exponential. It reminded her of the Compound Effect: if you doubled a penny every day for a month, in 30 days you'd have over $5 million.

Susan's earnings felt like that.

Soon after, she and her husband sold their other businesses. Their family thought they were crazy. But Susan and Murray were having the time of their lives. They traveled around the world building and developing networks. She created her own training tools and had a #1 training video. She led with the business opportunity and grew an amazing team of business builders. Countless people relied on her.

But the compensation plan proved too difficult to duplicate. By the time Susan's third team fell apart, the network marketing industry had broken her heart. She and her husband retired from the industry. Even though they had made a fortune, the failure rate was too high. She lost her belief in the network marketing model.

They left the industry for 15 years. And for 15 years, companies called her. Even I called Susan—who simply wasn't open, therefore she couldn't hear, that a compensation model could be generous, reliable, and pay your entire team.

Eventually, however, I convinced Susan to fly to our New Year Kickoff event where she fell in love with the network-marketing industry all over again. She'd forgotten how much she enjoyed the business, the community, and the "glass half full" kind of people you met. When she looked at the Isagenix compensation plan, she realized it was generous and simple—a perfect 10. *Build a network and we will pay you and YOUR TEAM,* Susan heard.

"I came back to the industry," Susan said, "because Isagenix had gotten the compensation model right."

She got amazing results herself on the Isagenix product, and began building a team like she'd never been away. Today, Susan's passion is to help professionalize this industry that she loves. She identifies potential leaders, then trains them to drive the line and build a sustainable network of their own.

What does Susan Miller know about team-building that you can learn and apply?

Let converging trends help you. Susan teaches her team to build their businesses based on trends that aren't going away. In fact, three trends in particular are not only converging on the world economy, but are dramatically impacting the network-marketing industry.

- *People's focus on health and wellness is on the rise.* They're seeking safe, dense nutrition vs. unsafe foods filled with harmful ingredients.

- *Entrepreneurship is on the rise, too.* Having a side hustle, working in the gig economy, and a desire for flexibility, time freedom, and more control over their income are driving an estimated 75% of the workforce, Susan says, to seek entrepreneurial opportunities by 2025. Millennials are a huge part of this movement. In fact, Bentley University, a leading business school in Massachusetts, surveyed college graduates—66% of whom said they wanted to work for themselves. Unfortunately, there are few types of businesses that a 22-year-old can start with no risk, except for network marketing which requires only time and knowledge.

- *Technology has made growing a network easier than ever.* From social media to video conferencing to downloadable tools and more, technology supports the most basic activity of network marketing: word-of-mouth and personal connections. Plus, it can happen all over the world for free.

Use a pencil pitch to explain the benefits of Isagenix. A "pencil pitch" is a quick one-on-one presentation you can use to share the financial benefits of Isagenix in about five to seven minutes. It only takes a blank piece of paper and a marking pen. And with practice, you can make the case for why network marketing—and Isagenix, in particular—is the ideal road map to personal wealth and financial certainty.

Susan Miller developed her pencil pitch based on the cash-flow model featured in the bestselling personal finance book, *Rich Dad Poor Dad,* by Robert Kiyosaki. We videotaped a 17-minute tutorial where Susan teaches how to deliver the pitch, as you draw the accompanying diagrams on blank paper. Check out the video online at the link below.*

One recommendation from Susan, however: before using this pencil pitch with anyone, read *The Business of the 21st Century,* by Robert Kiyosaki, which utilizes his cash-flow model for the Network Marketing Industry. The

---

* *See the video of Susan Miller's complete "pencil pitch" at* https://isagenixbusiness.com/learn-the-pencil-pitch-that-helped-this-former-hairdresser-build-a-team-of-isagenix-millionaires/

knowledge you gain will be helpful to you when explaining the four quadrants and Kiyosaki's cash-flow principles Susan features in her pitch.

Use the "top down" approach. Instead of presenting the Isagenix products first, Susan leads with the business opportunity. She identifies new business builders—people who are ambitious, coachable and pro-active—then invites them for further training. She casts a vision, then looks for interest. Often times, good leaders will self-identify: they're already doing the things that top earners do. Equipped with ability and a willingness to learn, Susan knows that good people only need to be connected with a role model to follow and a mentor who's built a team before.

Be a master team developer. Success is not about mass marketing... it's about mass duplication. Susan's goal is to build the strongest, most sustainable network possible.

She trains every morning on a different topic, Monday through Friday for 30 minutes. In the beginning, Susan did the training with just a handful of teammates. Now, they've developed many leaders, including Susan's husband and their 27-year-old daughter Chelsea, a START Ambassador, who does it with them. These team trainings not only teach duplicatable strategies and build community, they also give new leaders and their teams a safe space to learn the skills necessary to evolve to a professional network marketer themselves.

CHAPTER 7:

Do Good While Doing Well

*"You don't have to choose
between doing good
and doing well."*

—TIM COOK
Chief Executive Officer of Apple Inc.

One of the most rewarding results I see among the Isagenix family of associates is a legacy—not of finances—but of philanthropy. A legacy of willingness to help others with one's time, talent and treasures.

As Isagenix grew and prospered—as lives around the world were being changed—I wondered, *How else can we use this incredible nutrition that's been developed? How can we change the world by changing the next generation? How can we inspire people to take responsibility for their own health in addition to helping them recover when financial hardship occurs?*

Jim and I realized, as we and the company enjoyed greater success, that we had the means to answer these questions and help others less fortunate. Contributing to causes that are supportive to children was something we embraced early on. In fact, our first focus was to help children suffering from abuse. We started to give personally to Childhelp USA. Founded in 1959, it's the largest organization dedicated to helping victims of child abuse and neglect as well as at-risk children.

Later, we expanded our support to include the Make-a-Wish Foundation with more than $10 million in contributions from the Isagenix community towards granting children with life-threatening diseases the opportunity to have their wish come true.

Looking back, we were just getting started.

WHEN YOU FEEL GOOD, YOU DO GOOD

Once we were helping children—as well as helping people achieve their health and wellness goals—we looked for even more ways to further our dream of creating a healthier, happier world.

In 2018, we established the ISA Foundation, a nonprofit* organization whose mission is to create sustainable impact globally through volunteer efforts and charitable contributions focused on healthy nutrition and support for underserved children, wellness education for all, aid for those affected by natural disasters, and the pursuit of racial equality.

Isagenix covers all administrative costs of the Foundation so that 100% of donations can benefit those in need. In fact, the Foundation along with Isagenix has donated more than $15 million—including providing over four million nutritious meals to children and families in need around the world. As well, the Foundation has contributed to numerous disaster relief recovery projects worldwide.

Not only do many Isagenix Associates include the Foundation in their charitable giving, but we also look for other ways to support the Foundation's mission—including donating the proceeds from this book.

Of course, one of the projects that is watched and nurtured by the Isagenix Associates and corporate team is the company's grant to the Unstoppable Foundation which provides enhanced nutrition to small communities in Kenya, including: children getting healthy meals, support of community gardens, programs to improve healthy homes, and so much more related to getting nutritious food to those in need—many of whom are the local schoolchildren who are thriving with better nutrition.

Since 2014, Jim, Erik, Peta and I have personally supported the Unstoppable Foundation's "five pillar" approach to helping small villages thrive by providing education, clean water, nutritious food, healthcare, and income training. Additionally, when Erik and Peta were married, they dedicated their *givingmoon* to raising nearly $200,000 which positively impacted more than 2,000 villagers.

---

* *The ISA Foundation is a 501(c)3 nonprofit organization. For more information, visit* ISAFoundation.net.

BEING AN ENTREPRENEUR HELPS OTHERS, NOT JUST YOUR OWN BANK ACCOUNT

When you discover what you really want out of life...when you find your passion...when you decide what you truly love to do, that drive and conviction is inspiring to other people. Some of the most successful people in the world live out that drive and passion as entrepreneurs—business owners who, day after day, pursue their vision of success. That, too, is inspiring to others.

But beyond just inspiration, entrepreneurs have more opportunities at their fingertips to do good in the world. They can donate a portion of their earnings. They can practice sustainable sourcing of their products. They can even encourage their employees—as Isagenix does—to volunteer locally in their communities. Not a day goes by that I don't hear some news report about a small business (or a major corporation that was once a small business) creating good in the world by activating their time, talent and treasures.

You have the ability—and I believe you have the heart—to help a cause that you care about. When you do, you become a lifeline to others and a role model that your children, your team, and others can follow.

Your driven spirit will inspire others to do the same.

ANOTHER WAY TO DO GOOD:
PRACTICE SERVANT LEADERSHIP

One day I got a call from one of our associates. She was so excited about a new member whom she had just enrolled—a young woman who had so much drive and enthusiasm for Isagenix.

When I reached out to the young woman by phone, I could hear the excitement in her voice, the passion she had to succeed. Slowly, the magic begin to happen. She began going up the ladder and emerged as a leader.

Today, she has become a huge role model for Millennials in Isagenix. She has truly stepped into her power and is leading a huge team all around the world. Watching this woman's conviction and drive inspires everyone.

That's a wrap, said the morning show producer at the local TV network in Tampa. Emily Vavra smiled as she finished her on-air appearance, reflecting on her guest spot as a wellness expert before quickly turning her mind to the next gig coming up. That afternoon, she was scheduled to do a talk-show in Los Angeles on the topic of goal-setting.

Today, Emily loves her life.

Between leading her Isagenix team, volunteering at church, and speaking at business conferences where she shares the stage with icons like Harvey McKay, Emily Vavra is unstoppable, intentional and focused.

At 26, she was the youngest person ever to earn a million dollars at Isagenix. Plus she was named one of Yahoo's Top Ten Entrepreneurs to Watch 2020.

But life before Isagenix wasn't so glamorous.

Leaving home every morning at 5:00 a.m., Emily held down four different jobs—as a personal trainer, massage therapist, nanny and rehabilitation specialist for a plastic surgeon. She dragged herself home every night at 7:00 p.m., exhausted, yet still she was living paycheck to paycheck.

"I knew if I didn't find a way to make money while I was sleeping," Emily said, "I was going to be working forever."

One day at the gym, 23-year-old Emily realized she'd been watching another woman transform herself for nearly a year. The woman had released 90 pounds and started her own business. A former mortgage banker, she'd lost her job and had turned to Isagenix as her solution.

At the same time, Emily was suffering from low energy, binge eating and troublesome skin. Her stressful work life was beginning to show up in unpleasant ways. She wanted overall wellness—including financial wellness. She invited the woman to go for coffee and signed up for Isagenix right away.

Within days of beginning the Isagenix program, Emily started waking up before her alarm clock. She had more mental clarity, and her energy was off the charts. Soon, her bank account was looking better than ever, too.

She hit Executive rank in four months, and made $30,000 that first year. By age 24, she was making $100,000 annually—and by age 26, she'd brought home her first million. She'd become the youngest person to reach the title of Isagenix Millionaire in the history of the company.* Yet, today, she's more excited than ever about Isagenix. In fact, the most gratifying part of her life is helping other people achieve what she has done.

She's become a true servant leader.

"Putting other people's paychecks ahead of your own," says Emily, "making other people's goals and dreams and why's *more important* than your own is what servant leadership is all about."

For Emily, that means turning her focus toward being there for her team members every step of the way: helping them learn the necessary skills, getting on their first few calls, and enrolling people with them, not for them. But it also means leading by example, a philosophy that drives her to personally enroll 70 people per year. Along the way, she's built a culture of focus, personal growth and personal responsibility in her team. There's no drama—only activity that will evolve people into smart, successful individuals.

---

* Results not typical.

But most importantly, by being a servant leader herself, Emily is helping everyday people become leaders in their own right. She's created a safe space for people to grow. And when they do, the team celebrates with them. Whether it's losing a pound or earning their first $54 or doing their first home presentation, the team celebrates wins both big and small.

As Emily explains, "Everything rises and falls on leadership."

One of the hallmarks of Emily's organization is a discipline she calls *total immersion:* working with others in the network to help everyone stay focused and active.

"It means keeping Isagenix at the front of your mind," says Emily. "It becomes part of the fabric of your life. You focus on it. And what you focus on expands."

Her team's *Total Immersion Formula* includes seven core commitments:

- Achieve two to five exposures a day to keep your business in play.
- Focus on rank advancement to grow people and grow your team. When are you going for your next goal, and who are you helping to get to theirs?
- Participate in weekly training with Emily to build your skills.
- Commit to weekly presentations—either watching online, attending someone else's or hosting your own—to practice enrolling.
- Read at least 10 pages a day of a self-help book to improve your confidence, skills, and motivation.
- Attend major Isagenix events including Celebration, the company's global conference held annually.
- And finally, commit to being here one year from now.

As a result of these commitments, Emily Vavra's team has had the best event attendance in Isagenix. And their commitment to business success has created the time and resources for members to also give back to the world and special populations in need. They regularly volunteer locally, at church and through mission trips, as well as help fund ISA Foundation initiatives.

"Do what is easy and your life will be hard.
Do what is hard and your life will become easy."

—LES BROWN

Bestselling author, motivational speaker, and talk-show host

CAST A WIDE NET AND BRING OTHERS ALONG WITH YOU

One day, rumblings began at the office about a woman from the East Coast who was setting New Jersey and New York on fire. Jim and I travelled to that area to do an event and, when we arrived, there was a line outside with about 400 people waiting to get in. Inside, more than 600 people were already seated.

Who was behind all this team spirit?

As the meeting started, an inspirational lady came to the front and shared how Isagenix had changed her life. We were blown away by the other stories that were shared that night, too: bartenders, dancers, mechanics…all were having life-changing experiences because this one amazing woman had said yes to Isagenix.

Shy and reserved, Alexis Romano spent 21 years as an English teacher and high school counselor. Though she had a Master's degree—and numerous advanced certificates—she never made the kind of income she dreamed about. She worked extra jobs: tutoring, waitressing, even cleaning beach houses during the summer. By working harder, she told herself, she'd get more out of life.

But the "more" she craved hadn't shown up yet.

In August of 2008, when teachers and administrators returned to school after summer break, Alexis immediately noticed the Vice-Principal—a friend—looked better than ever. *What's he been doing?* she wondered.

When he told her about Isagenix, she was skeptical. Still, Alexis researched the company and decided to start on the products. Like a lot of people, she didn't want stuff shipped to her house every 30 days. *But that viewpoint changed a mere three days later.* Her energy had skyrocketed, her sleep patterns had improved, and she had also lost nine pounds.

Attending her first Isagenix event, she saw a teacher step onto the stage to share his story. *If he could do it,* Alexis thought, *then I can, too.* In fact, the opportunity built into the Isagenix compensation plan seemed endless to her. Finally, she believed she could build the kind of income she wanted.

But even Alexis admits that she was not an overnight success.

In her first year, she earned $7,000—a nice extra sum for a schoolteacher on a budget—and, in her second year, she nearly doubled that. It was a far cry from her educator's salary, but she could see her team growing. *Be consistent,* Alexis told herself. *Be persistent.*

By the time another two years went by, she had almost matched her teacher's salary. Within months, she gave up her teaching job, walked away from her benefits package, and settled for less than her fully vested pension—knowing her Isagenix business would pay off even more in the future. Just one year later, Alexis Romano earned a stunning $900,000 in personal income from the network that she had built.*

She was an ordinary person who'd become extraordinary in the process.

But more importantly, along the way, she had cast a wide net and enrolled everyday people with their own dreams and goals—plus hardships to overcome. She enrolled mom-preneurs and musicians and fellow educators and fitness instructors. Together, Alexis and her teammates are changing lives.

She understands that this business is not about your own situation—how much weight you've lost or haven't lost . . . how much money you're making

---

* *Results not typical.*

or not making. It's about something magical we have that transforms lives both physically and financially.

"You're doing people a disservice by not talking about Isagenix." Alexis teaches her team. "Get grounded and build your belief in this formula we have, so you can go out and transform people's lives."

"You can have everything in life you want,
if you will just help other people
get what they want."

—ZIG ZIGLAR
World renowned speaker and author of
30 books including See You at the Top

"I HAVE THE TIME AND RESOURCES TO DO SOMETHING BIGGER THAN ME"

One day, I got a call from Jani Ehlo. She was over the moon with excitement about a new lady on her team: Jessica Reigner. Jani quickly put me in touch, and the energy that came through the phone was off the charts.

Jessica wanted it all—everything Isagenix had to offer. Today, she leads a huge team and many of them text me. *There is no one like Jessica,* they say. *Her conviction is so infectious. She has helped me so much.*

She is a true leader who excites and inspires everyone in Isagenix.

"How much would it take to make it worth your time?" said the stranger on the other end of the phone. Taken aback, Jessica Reigner thought deeply for a moment.

Just getting this phone call reminded her vaguely of a late-night movie where two gangsters were sizing each other up. *And how had this Isagenix associate even found her to begin with?* After all, Jessica was a Vice President and Managing Director at Citibank.

Corporate Sales, no less.

Her department was in charge of processing billions of dollars' worth of paychecks to millions of distributors in network marketing companies around the globe. As an insider, she saw the good, the bad, and the ugly of the industry. She knew what was behind every curtain.

And there was no question… Isagenix was the best.

It had the best compensation plan. And she knew people needed the products. But more than that, Isagenix was the best at putting their associates first. *If it's not right for the associates,* she'd been told when she'd tried to negotiate extra fees on behalf of Citibank, *it's not right for the company.*

But now Jessica was faced with an interesting question: would becoming an Isagenix associate *herself* bring about the kind of lifestyle Jessica really wanted? After all, she traveled a lot, worked long hours, and her young daughter—who was in the care of Jessica's live-in nanny—was growing up way too fast. Turning her mind back to the woman on the phone, Jessica gave the question some serious thought.

She's either insane or she's brilliant. I have to find out which.

Starting fast and working hard, in her first 26 months as an Isagenix associate, Jessica made a staggering one million dollars. It wasn't typical, she knew, but it was a blessing to her family. She finally had the financial resources and the time freedom to be the best mom possible.[*]

At a Monday evening Isagenix event, another mom on Jessica's team announced she had adopted a drug-exposed baby boy, Gabriel. Her story inspired Jessica on a very deep level.

What if, thought Jessica. Living on the outskirts of Philadelphia, she'd seen the need for safe housing and loving care for thousands of abandoned foster children. The stories of violence and abuse were heart-breaking.

---

[*] *Results not typical.*

Right now, she said to herself, *I have the time and resources to do something bigger than me.*

Over the past five years, Jessica and her husband Doug have fostered nine different children. They brought a baby boy home from the hospital at just five days old. They've fostered siblings, including a sister who was blind and never knew what she looked like until the Reigners told her how beautiful she was. They took in a two-year-old girl and her six-year-old brother who were found sleeping in a car on a freezing Philadelphia night.

Today, Jessica and Doug have three biological children, one adopted child and two foster children living in their household. They're now on their ninth placement, working with local county resources and birth families to reunite children in a safe and loving environment.

The positive impact on their family—and especially their biological children—has been profound. They've become more compassionate. They understand the consequences when adults make bad decisions. And they've learned what it's like to step in and help when it's simply easier to say no.

Isagenix has given Jessica not only the time freedom and financial resources to step into the role of a foster mom, it's given her a platform to attract other foster parents to Isagenix—and inspire Isagenix associates to become foster and adoptive parents themselves.

Today, the Adoptagenix movement—started by Deanna Falchook and a handful of other Isagenix associates—includes thousands of families blessed by adoption who are coming together to build healthy and prosperous forever families.

---

*"I think there is something to be said
for what you can do when you don't know what
you aren't supposed to be able to do."*

—LIZ MURRAY
*Teacher and motivational speaker accepted to
Harvard University as a teenager despite being homeless*

WHAT'S THE EXTRAORDINARY THING
THAT YOU'RE SUPPOSED TO DO?

By giving associates time freedom, a global reach, and the ability to become financially confident in their future, Isagenix also gives them something else: the confidence they need to let their natural generosity shine.

As Isagenix expands the meaning of "doing good while doing well," associates from around the globe are partnering with us to improve not only their own lives, but the lives of people in need, as well.

And that's a future I'm excited about.

CONCLUSION: THE FUTURE

We have a saying here at Isagenix: "Start a healthy change in this world, right now. It all starts with you!"

When Jim, John and I first started this journey as Isagenix's founding members, we had a vision for the company: we wanted to be known as the company who has the healthiest people on the planet, pays out the most in our compensation plan, and has a lot of fun.

But that was just a precursor to what this company would actually become.

It reminds me that everything we do in life prepares us for the future. Just as I spent years in my career before co-founding this company, Isagenix has spent years establishing its reputation as the world's premier health and wellness company. And the best is yet to come. In fact, we're advancing every day to help even more people improve their own wellness, face global health challenges, lessen the stress of financial hardship, and thrive in every way. Living the good life isn't about just material wealth—it's a combination of health, financial certainty, and surrounding yourself with a supportive, positive community of people who care about your future.

Isagenix is that future.

Now, with a new decade upon us, we're completely reinventing Isagenix to stay ahead of the curve and meet the modern demands of a population that wants to live longer and enjoy life more. When people don't have good health or financial wellbeing, they're simply not able to enjoy the full measure of what life has to offer.

To meet the demand, we're pursuing a three-point initiative called Isagenix 2.0.

First, we're upgrading our core products to leverage both scientific advances and modern food technology including using more raw food ingredients and lowering the sugar content. At the same time, we'll be streamlining our product portfolio to focus on enhancing product categories that better speak to who we are as a company.

Secondly, we're evolving our marketing, branding and messaging to elevate the total Isagenix experience—from the packaging you open to the experience of our live events to every other touchpoint imaginable. You'll feel extra good about being involved with the company. And you'll be pampering yourself in Insta-worthy ways that you can't wait to share with others.

And, third, we're upgrading the customer experience by making huge enhancements in technology. We're upgrading our online platform, developing new apps, and creating new ways for people to purchase Isagenix products. Additionally, in January 2020, we eliminated our membership fee which not only makes it easier for people to purchase, it has also opened the floodgates for new consumers to try a few starter products versus buying larger packages. Plus, as an Isagenix associate, you'll have easier and more intuitive access to reports and information of all kinds to help you grow your business.

Of course, the backbone of Isagenix will always be our amazing compensation plan, which we've continually upgraded for the past 18 years. As part of Isagenix 2.0, we want to provide new ways to do business and even better ways to pay people for focusing on growing their independent Isagenix business.

YOUR FUTURE IS UP TO YOU.
BUT ISAGENIX HAS THE ANSWER.

Not only is this revolution inside Isagenix designed to support millions more Isagenix associates than we have now, it's designed to support an individual family's own journey toward better health and wellness.

And it can't come a moment too soon.

It's clear that every household needs to take responsibility for their own immunity and financial stability. Eliminating toxins, consuming a *nutrient-dense, lower calorie diet,* reducing the stress of work-life imbalance, and creating a side income are just a few things you can do to take charge of your future and thrive in the face of widespread declining health, economic turmoil, and cataclysmic shifts in labor markets. As humans, we also need to lower our risk profile by reducing obesity, controlling our sugar intake and preventing adult-onset diabetes, and getting better quality sleep. At the same time, we need to optimize our financial future, reduce the stress of financial uncertainty, and create a less worrying way to make a living—even it means just adding a side hustle to a current job.

Sometimes things come along in life that change everything. The evolution of the gig economy and the resulting economic upheaval has been the greatest disrupter in recent times. It's situations like these when we should ask ourselves, *Do I have a plan in place to support the lifestyle I want for myself and my family—both now and into the future?*

Isagenix is a way to create a safer income that's not just based on your own efforts, but on the collective efforts of others, too. Instead of being one of millions of unemployed people that fall victim to an economic crisis, you have the opportunity to create an income that's not dependent upon showing up for a job—or whether your employer is even still in business.

Your physical and financial future is up to you. Isagenix has the answer.

"Outstanding people have one thing in common:
an absolute sense of mission."

—ZIG ZIGLAR
World renowned speaker and author of
30 books including See You at the Top

WHAT'S YOUR PERSONAL MISSION?

I believe I was put on this planet to make a difference, and it is my life mission to support others in transforming their lives—both physically and financially.

You, too, can have a personal mission that inspires every decision you make and commands every action you take. Having a strong vision of your future is key. When you know *why you're doing what you're doing,* it will drive your success. If you have the right intent, the magic will happen.

As a family—and as the guardians of Isagenix's future—our vision is to impact world health and free people from physical and financial pain, and in the process, create the most trusted and respected health and wellness company in the world.

Notice I didn't say "create the *largest* company." Why?

As Erik explains, "It's all about where you focus. Though we always strive to reach more people and change as many lives as possible, the terms *largest* and *biggest* don't always set up a company to be the most trusted or to make the most impact. Far from it. In fact, the business decisions around becoming the *biggest* look a lot different from those that further the goal of becoming the *most trusted* and *most respected.* If we focus on those two things, then growing and expanding to become the largest health and wellness company will take care of itself."

Creating better products, being more transparent in our messaging, and finding new ways to benefit our customers and associates are what Erik brings to these high level decisions. He wants Isagenix to not only be a household name, but also to be part of the conversation around living a healthy lifestyle—an iconic brand that makes people feel empowered.

"When people go to buy a smartphone, they think of Apple," Erik says. "When people go to buy running shoes, they think of Nike. In five to ten years, when people think about living a long and healthy life, I want them to turn to Isagenix."

Our biggest competition is not another company, he continues. Our biggest foe is the mindset that people have no control over their health and have to reach for a prescription drug to maintain their health instead. Changing that mindset is not only possible, it's become Erik's own personal mission inside the company.

"Man never made any material as resilient as the human spirit."

—BERNARD WILLIAMS
Author of Making Sense of Humanity

STAY FOCUSED, BE RESILIENT AND THRIVE

Of course, vibrant good health is only part of living your best life. There's so much more to the formula. It takes focus and determination. Plus, it's not enough to merely survive this life—the goal is to thrive.

Here are some other ways you can stay resilient, succeed and prosper:

Do what you love to do. Know what drives you. Identify what gets you excited. I love to help people enjoy the best health ever with our products and nutritional system, but what also inspires me is watching lives change with the Isagenix business opportunity. I see mothers staying home with their children and helping other moms do the same. It gives me so much joy that it drives me every day to do more and to give more so I can help others achieve their dreams.

Focus on bringing value to others. I always ask our independent members, "How can I serve you? How can I help you achieve your dreams?" It takes some of them by surprise that I am so invested in their success, but I have always been passionate about servant leadership, so helping people reach their goals is top-of-mind for me.

Surround yourself with a good team. Find people who have the skills that you don't have, so you all complement each other. At Isagenix, having the right people on our Executive Leadership Team allows our executives to learn from each other, which raises everyone's standing within their professions. In the same way, you can build an organization where top talent brings their best selves—and their best ideas—to the team as a whole. This not only goes for your business, but for your family and inner circle of friends, as well.

Stay current in your skills. We all need to stay relevant in the marketplace, and having a professional online presence is crucial. If you haven't mastered the complexities of social media, webinars, and other aspects of the digital revolution, seek out people to help you get up to speed. The same goes for communications, marketing, and technology.

Live within your means. Stick to a budget and take on bigger household expenses only when you're *very certain* of your income. I've seen so many Isagenix leaders (and entrepreneurs, in general) expand their lifestyle with expensive houses, fast cars and luxury travel before they've put their financial house in order. The reality is that financial certainty is your responsibility and comes from *financial preparedness*—plus living within your means. What can you do? Pay down your debt. Fund your children's college education. Work with a professional to create a solid investment plan. Pare down unnecessary expense. When all that's done, *then* reward yourself with the comfortable lifestyle you deserve.

> *"The most important skill you need is the ability to learn how to change and grow."*
>
> —SCOTT COOK
> *Billionaire co-founder of financial software giant Intuit*

ALWAYS BE GROWING...*YOURSELF*

In my lifetime, I've made a constant study of the best advice from experts in the human-potential field. Not only does their advice on personal growth empower me to constantly improve, it keeps me inspired about my ability to do so. When I read stories of courageous people who've overcome the odds to achieve some miraculous goal, I realize there is no obstacle so great that I cannot achieve what I want, too—for myself, for my family, and for the worldwide movement that Isagenix has become.

This kind of inspiration and knowledge is also available to you.

When you read a report about the latest health study, or pick up a book on brain science, or sit in on a webinar about entrepreneurship, you not only stay current with where the world is going, but you'll be reminded that *you already have everything you need within yourself* to achieve the greatest of goals. Through books, white papers, articles and podcasts, you have access to the greatest thinkers of our day. Make them a part of your journey.

What we focus on tends to expand and improve. So commit to constant and never-ending improvement. In the end, the life we have lived is a direct result of the decisions we've made, the knowledge we've acquired, and the actions we've taken.

Always be learning. Never stop achieving.

NEVER GIVE UP ON YOUR DREAMS

I truly hope this book has helped open the possibility in your own life to dream...to learn...to take action...and to never give up on your dreams. As I lay my head on my pillow every night—with so much gratitude that we are making an impact—I'm also grateful for the amazing leaders we have in the company who really want to make a difference in this world. I'm so proud of their accomplishments. They pour their hearts into helping others, and it's such a beautiful thing to see. In fact, the collective energy and actions of our associates, customers, and management team is exciting to watch and keeps me inspired every day.

I'm also excited about the thousands upon thousands of moms who get to stay at home with their children, yet still make an income to fulfill their dreams. For all the children who have their parents with them throughout the day: what a gift. I'm excited about the people who can help their parents as they age and be with them in time of need. And I'm excited about the families who can make an extra $500 to $1,000 a month—often the thing that keeps them from bankruptcy or divorce.

I'm excited that we've given hope and belief to people that they can have control of their health. They can live a life of energy and fulfillment.

And I'm excited by the young entrepreneurs who are joining our community and looking towards a future of fun, contribution and freedom.

I'm grateful for my family. They have supported me and inspired me. Jim, Erik, and Peta—you have been my rock.

In the end, our dreams can inspire us to a life beyond anything we can possibly imagine in the moment. I've discovered that the future is what *we make it.* This is what drives me every day to do more. I know it's why I was put on this planet.

ABOUT THE AUTHOR

Co-Founder and Executive Vice President of Isagenix International, LLC, Kathy Coover is well-known in the industry as one of the Most Influential Women in Direct Selling. Her career spans more than 28 years and includes achieving her goal of becoming the top income earner at three separate network marketing companies. In 2002, she decided to join forces with her husband, Jim, to form Isagenix and has spent the last two decades helping countless families reshape their financial future and regain a healthier outlook on life. In 2015, the American Business Awards honored Kathy with its prestigious Woman of the Year award because of her unwavering commitment to always help others.

Having started her professional career as a dental hygienist, Kathy understands firsthand what it's like to work 40-plus hours a week. It wasn't until Jim suggested she try network marketing that she realized she could still financially contribute to the family household while also staying home with their son, Erik, who was a toddler at the time. It was then that she became passionate about sharing direct selling's flexible work-life model with other women and families. Kathy's personal mission is to be an advocate for women and empower all families to live their best lives.

Creating a Lasting Legacy

For future generations, including her own grandchildren, Kathy wants to ensure the legacy she and Jim have created in Isagenix is around forever. Her hope is that Isagenix will always be looked up to for its commitment to doing the right thing and making a difference in communities around the world.

PERMISSIONS

WORDS THAT INSPIRE
ME TO DO MORE

There's no question that being in an executive leadership role—as a co-founder of Isagenix and as a 28-year industry veteran—has its rewards. But nothing is more rewarding, inspiring and motivating to me than the individuals and families who are being uplifted and changed every day through Isagenix products and the Isagenix business opportunity.

When I receive letters and notes of thanks like the sampling featured below, it reminds me why I strive every day . . . and why I'm always inspired to do more.

I am not sure where to begin in expressing exactly how impressed I was all weekend by you and your company. Your own personal commitment to the vision and mission of Isagenix is not only obvious, but commendable. …Thank you for your hospitality, generosity, and professionalism. However, more importantly, thank you for your authenticity. As one who longs and loves to connect with others at a core level, I so appreciate a woman of your stature being so incredibly grounded, open, and just real.

—Zach

Dear Kathy,

This company is changing my life, inside and out. I feel GREAT! It feels like I am turning back the clock to the young woman I was, coming out of graduate school. I was filled with hope and belief that making a difference was not just possible, it was my mission in life. Over the years, life happened and my light dimmed. My confidence in myself and in others dropped.

And then I was introduced to this community of fantastic people all taking an awesome product—sharing and enriching the lives others—while getting rich along the way. I feel so blessed to have been introduced to this company. My level of confidence is up, and my light is much brighter than it has been in awhile.

This company has encouraged me to step into my power and not play small, while helping others do the same. It has encouraged me to listen to others, find out what they need and then be of service. I have seen lives shift back to peace and happiness. Wow, I know there is so much more to come, and I welcome it all with open arms.

—Anonymous

Thank you so very much for serving and giving your heart to our executives today! It meant the world to me! You truly are the biggest inspiration, and I am forever grateful for you. Everyone is fired up, and we are ready to run!! Thank you for showing me what's possible. Isagenix saved my family and has given me a bigger purpose, and I commit to following your vision always and forever!

—Abby

I just wanted to send you a thank you for all you do. This opportunity has changed my entire family's life. Both my parents are having severe health challenges, and if it wasn't for Isagenix, I don't know where we would be. I'm able to be there for them emotionally and financially and my sister as well. I am grateful every day, and every time I'm in the hospital with one of my parents, I'm reminded of how grateful I am and what a priceless opportunity this is. Thank you always. I am forever grateful. Love you.

—Alexis

Dear Kathy,

I just want to take a moment to recognize you for your dedication to the members of Isagenix. You continually amaze us as you pour yourself into the company with your energy, love and knowledge. Your desire to share and help people change their lives is a gift through you from God. Thank you for all you do. May God continue to bless you.

—Marti

Thank you for leading the way.

Thank you for being all heart.

Thank you for being a visionary.

Thank you for doing the hard things to make what is already great even more extraordinary.

Thank you for being genuine.

Thank you for caring so much about each and every one of your extended family.

Thank you for always dreaming bigger.

Thank you for never quitting.

I love and appreciate you.

I am honored and blessed to be a part of the best company family in the world.

—Dr. Corey

Thanks for Being You . . .

I am honored to be a part of your Isa Family. You lead with integrity and do things because it is the right thing to do without any hidden agenda. Thank you for pouring your heart and soul into the company. You are amazing role models who lead with their hearts. I am truly blessed to be on this journey to impact world health and free people from physical and financial pain.

Gratefully yours,
Bonnie

Kathy,

You and Jim have changed my life in a way that made it possible to be a full time mom and have a career that fits my lifestyle. You allowed me to dream; you allowed me to stretch way beyond my comfort zone and created a foundation of belief that "Anything is Possible"!

Your leadership has inspired me to share this vision for those that welcome change and opportunity to their lives.

Thank you for coming to Spokane last year. It meant so much to meet the two of you in person and to share the Isagenix vision of changing lives one person at a time.

Thank you for the time spent at dinner with Dr Cheryle Hart and Ron Grossman last month at the Isagenix University. It has propelled them to join this team and take us to the next level. Dr. Hart is committed to the Isagenix vision as well. Your personal touch validated the sincerity of two CEO's willing to go the distance for the new members to feel the passion and purpose of this great company. As you can see they won the cruise last week and are looking forward to celebrating with all of you in March.

Thank you once again for your leadership and dedication to the Isagenix family. I am honored to be one of the 2008 Women of Isagenix!

If there is ever anything I can do for you, please don't hesitate to call upon me.

With sincere gratitude,
Carol

WE BELIEVE

EVERY CHILD DESERVES A
HEALTHY, NUTRITIOUS MEAL.

EVERY PERSON DESERVES THE
EDUCATION AND EMPOWERMENT
TO LIVE A HEALTHY LIFE.

EVERY FAMILY DESERVES TO
SURVIVE AND RECOVER FROM
A NATURAL DISASTER.

EVERYONE DESERVES EQUAL
TREATMENT, REGARDLESS OF RACE.

ISA FOUNDATION
Inspire. Share. Advocate.

WHEN YOU FEEL BETTER, YOU DO BETTER.

Along with helping people achieve their health and wellness goals,
giving back has always been at the core of the Isagenix mission.
The ISA Foundation is the culmination of that mission as well as our
dream of creating a healthier, happier world.

For more information, visit ISAFoundation.net.

Proceeds from this book will be donated to the ISA Foundation to support its mission.

Established in 2018, the ISA Foundation is a 501(c)(3) nonprofit organization whose mission is to create sustainable impact globally through volunteer efforts and charitable contributions focused on healthy nutrition and support for underserved children, wellness education for all, aid for those affected by natural disasters, and the pursuit of racial equality. Isagenix International covers all administrative costs of the foundation so 100% of donations can benefit those in need. Through 2020, the ISA Foundation has awarded a total of $3.25 million in grants, which included funding to provide over 4 million nutritious meals to children and families in need around the world.